Writing in Preschool

Learning to Orchestrate Meaning and Marks

Judith A. Schickedanz
Boston University
Boston, Massachusetts, USA

Renée M. Casbergue
University of New Orleans
New Orleans, Louisiana, USA

INTERNATIONAL
Reading Association
800 BARKSDALE ROAD, PO BOX 8139
NEWARK, DE 19714-8139, USA
www.reading.org

KH

Editorial Director, Books and Special Projects   Matthew W. Baker
Managing Editor   Shannon T. Fortner
Permissions Editor   Janet S. Parrack
Acquisitions and Communications Coordinator   Corinne M. Mooney
Associate Editor, Books   Charlene M. Nichols
Administrative Assistant   Michele Jester
Assistant Permissions Editor   Tyanna L. Collins
Production Department Manager   Iona Muscella
Supervisor, Electronic Publishing   Anette Schütz
Electronic Publishing Specialist   R. Lynn Harrison
Proofreader   Elizabeth C. Hunt

Project Editors   Matthew W. Baker and Shannon T. Fortner

Freelance Editor   Susan Hodges

Cover Design   Linda Steere

Web addresses in this book were correct as of the publication date but may have become inactive or otherwise modified since that time. If you notice a deactivated or changed Web address, please e-mail books@reading.org with the words "Website Update" in the subject line. In your message, specify the Web link, the book title, and the page number on which the link appears.

Library of Congress Cataloging-in-Publication Data
Schickedanz, Judith A., 1944–
    Writing in preschool : learning to orchestrate meaning and marks / Judith A. Schickedanz, Renée M. Casbergue.
        p. cm.
    Includes bibliographical references and index.
    ISBN 0-87207-546-X
    1. Language arts (Preschool).   2. English language—Composition and exercises—Study and teaching (Preschool) I. Casbergue, Renee Michelet   II. Title.
    LB1140.5.L3S39 2004
    372.62'3--dc22
                                                                                      2004015527

Third Printing, October 2005

10/19/06

CONTENTS

GLOSSARY

The following glossary provides definitions for many of the specialized literacy terms in this book. These terms are highlighted in boldface type the first time they appear in each chapter.

alphabetic principle: The understanding that letters of the alphabet are used to represent the sounds heard in words. Prior to developing the alphabetic principle, children use letters randomly as visual icons.

directionality: Understanding about the left-to-right, top-to-bottom convention of placing English writing on a page.

discovery center: A tabletop area in a classroom stocked with nature (e.g., shells, rocks, and nests) and other items (e.g., magnifying lenses) for children to handle and observe.

dramatic play: An advanced form of play in which children take on roles and act out make-believe stories and situations.

mock letters: Designs made with lines found in standard alphabet letters, but composed to create a unique symbol that is not a standard letter (e.g., an *E* with five horizontal lines, not three).

mock words: Arrangements of letters that closely follow the *look* of actual words, even though they do not represent real words in the English language.

nonphonemic letter strings: A series of letters used by children to represent words without consideration of the sounds represented by those letters. Children use nonphonemic letter strings to approximate conventional writing based on its appearance.

oral language: Communication based on speech.

phonemic awareness: The awareness of the sounds (phonemes) that make up spoken words.

phonological awareness: The awareness of the constituent sounds of words in learning to read and spell.

symbolic resources: Occasions for writing that occur routinely in the classroom or at home and are internalized by the child, such that, in time, their performance requires little or no prompting by adults.

writing center: A classroom area stocked with materials that invite children to engage in writing.

CHAPTER 1

Where Young Children Start in Learning to Write

• • • • • • • • • • • • • • •

As another day begins, children arrive at their preschool. Four-year-old Gretchen is standing in the doorway, head bowed, eyes aimed at the floor. Her mother, standing close behind, nudges her gently and says, "Go ahead. Tell your teacher."

Gretchen raises her head as she walks through the doorway. "I got stitches," she announces, as she turns her head to expose the right side of her chin. Her teacher looks and also notices a bruise above her right eye. "What happened, Gretchen?" her teacher asks in a concerned tone. "I falled," Gretchen explains.

"You fell? Did you fall someplace at your house, or did you fall at the park across the street?"

"In my room," Gretchen replies. "And I can't jump on my bed anymore."

"Oh, you fell while jumping on your bed?" her teacher asks.

"I falled on the rocking chair," Gretchen offers.

"Oh, you fell off your bed while jumping on it, and you hit the rocking chair?" her teacher asks.

"I can't jump on the rocking chair anymore," Gretchen says.

"You didn't try to jump from your bed to a rocking chair, did you?" her teacher asks in an incredulous tone. Gretchen nods "Yes."

"Oh, my. No wonder you fell. So, you tried to jump into a rocking chair, and then what happened?"

"I, I, like this (uses hand motions to trace trajectory of fall), and then the…the…the rocking chair…the rocking chair, like this (uses hands again to indicate object falling over), and the thing on the…that thing on the…on the bottom…the chair, the rocking chair hit my eye (hand up to eye) and my chin bumped the floor and bleeded (hand on chin), and then my Mommy came and I had to sit in my car seat for the hospital."

"So, you jumped up off the bed, tried to land in the seat of the rocking chair, and then the rocking chair fell over, with you in it. When the rocking chair fell over, you fell onto the floor, and the rocking chair, maybe the bottom part, the part that makes the chair rock, hit you in the eye, and then your chin hit the floor?"

"Yes, yes, and then I had to…had to…had to go to the hospital and they did stitches. My mommy took me."

"Yes, your mommy came to your room and then she took you to the hospital."

"Yes, and my brother."

"Oh, your brother went too. Well, I'm sorry that you hurt yourself and had to have stitches. I bet you were scared."

"Yes, I was."

"That would be a wonderful story for our class book," says the teacher. "Maybe you'd like to draw some pictures and I could write down what you say about what happened. Then, we could add this story to our class book. What do you think?"

Gretchen does not answer. By this time, several children have gathered around to listen to the news, and Gretchen's best friend is clutching her hand. The children head to a table to play and to continue to talk about Gretchen's adventure of the night before.

● ● ● ● ● ● ● ● ● ● ● ● ● ● ● ●

Gretchen's experience was a topic of conversation several times throughout the day, and other children told of similar experiences and of trips to the hospital. A hospital theme emerged in the **dramatic play** center. Some children took the role of parents, as they called the doctor, took sick children to the hospital, and warned about dangerous activities such as jumping on beds, running out into the street, or getting lost in a store. As the children played, they created stories, pulling from their own experience to create fictionalized scenarios for themselves, other players, and dolls that served as "babies."

As the school year progressed, this fictionalization of personal experience became a central theme in children's play and writing. By the end of the year, children had a large repertoire of processed experiences from which to draw, some skill in weaving events together, and genuine interest in using writing to preserve and share their ideas.

One book, composed by a team of two young 5-year-olds (a few months older than 5 years), a combined firefighting, a favorite play theme of one author, with knowledge about the role of doctors in treating injuries. The pair composed the story together aloud and took turns drawing pictures on the pages of a blank book they found in the classroom **writing center**. Later, using the illustrations to prompt their recall, the students retold the story to a teacher who wrote it down and later typed it on strips for each page. The task of transcribing the story would have overwhelmed such young children. Knowing that they could anchor their composition with pictures and enlist the teacher to record the words gave them the latitude they needed to spin quite a tale.

In the story, a young boy suffers a series of injuries, each of which requires a visit to a doctor's office. Here's the first problem, and how the doctor solved it:

> Four lollipops were on fire.
>
> A little boy ate one lollipop and his tongue caught on fire.
>
> Then, he had to go see the doctor at the doctor's office.
>
> The doctor poked a hose in the little boy's mouth to put out the fire.
>
> (Excerpt from *FIRE FIRE*, composed by two young 5-year-olds)

But no sooner had the boy recovered from his burned tongue than he tripped on a stone, hit his mouth, and knocked out all his teeth. The young boy put his teeth under his pillow that night, and the tooth fairy left $20. Unfortunately, the boy had two more accidents the next day. His mom forgot to take her purse to the doctor this time, and the child had to pay the doctor with his own $20 bill. That night, the boy wished on a star that he would have no more bad luck and would somehow get more $20 bills. After that, we are told that he had no more bad luck and that he got another $20 bill. (We don't know from where.) He bought an ice cream cone with some of the money, but the ice cream fell out of the cone. Then, suddenly, it was Christmas, the boy was happy again because he received lots of presents, and the story ends.

Composing Without Writing/ Writing Without Composing

Gretchen never composed a second account of her fall and stitches for her teacher to record in the class book. At 4 years of age, there is a strong desire to *tell* all about something but little desire to create a record of the experience once the story has been told. Preschoolers have yet to discover how written records help people recall and share their past experiences. We saw earlier that Gretchen fictionalized her experience in dramatic play but did not record the experience on paper. Nonetheless, she was learning to compose a story—an essential element of writing—and her teacher knew how to help her develop this important writing skill.

The preschool child also creates a large quantity of writing that has no specific message, as seen in Figure 1. Figure 1a shows the work of a 4-year-old. When asked what the writing said, he replied, "Nothing." Figure 1b is a page from a 14-page storybook written by a 4-year-old, but the story has no content. Figure 1c is a practice piece: A child experimented with making a lot of letterlike forms and actual letters. The strings of letters in Figure 1d are "words," but not any words in particular. They are **mock words**—the products of the 4-year-old's experimentation with word making. Experimenting with form, devoid of message, helps children develop writing skill.

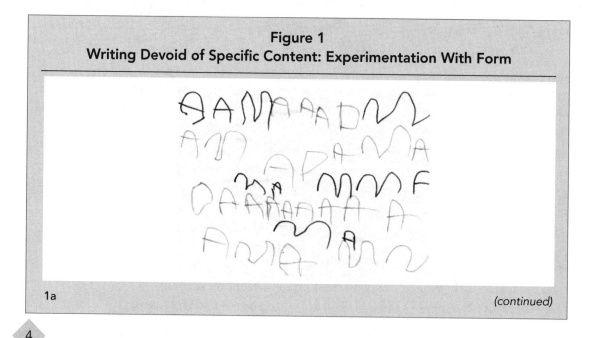

Figure 1
Writing Devoid of Specific Content: Experimentation With Form

1a

(continued)

Figure 1 (continued)

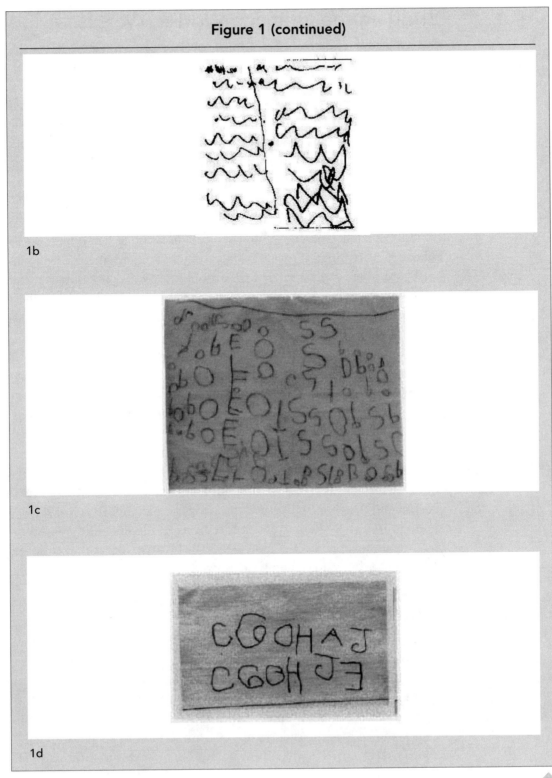

1b

1c

1d

5

Bridging the Oral and Written Worlds

The preschool teacher watches from a front-row seat as children acquire beginning understandings about writing and takes a leading role in helping children bridge worlds that they cannot at first connect by themselves. As we saw with Gretchen, there is the world of thoughts and feelings, and the world of oral language that the child uses to express them. Like Gretchen, preschoolers cannot at first tell us their stories all on their own. "I got stitches," she said initially, and then, "I falled." Gradually, in response to her teacher's genuine interest and concern, Gretchen was able to tell the whole story.

There are also worlds of marks that can preserve the stories children compose and tell. Using marks to create pictures comes fairly naturally to children, even though, given their rudimentary drawing skill, young preschoolers often must interpret their pictures for us. As children move through the preschool years, pictures become better able to stand on their own to convey a child's meaning. As skill in creating marks grows, so does a child's ability to convey a message.

Using marks to create print develops alongside the development of children's picture-making skill, between 3 and 5 years of age. Skill in creating print forms (i.e., designs that are alphabet letters, and strings of letters that look like words), however, does not lead directly to skill in expressing meaning. It's a different kind of development—a different strand—one that needs the kind of support that Gretchen's teacher provided.

For a long time, young children need to tell us what their writing says—what it means. Their writing simultaneously resides in two worlds, the oral and the written. Beginning during the preschool years and continuing through kindergarten, children very gradually build an understanding of how print actually works. Little by little, marks that children put on a page begin to stand on their own.

Journey Across the Bridges

This book, intended for teachers of 3-, 4-, and young 5-year-old children, describes the preschool child's journey in learning to write and the preschool teacher's important contributions to that journey. The stories of several journeys will be told, because the child's writing development rests on the gradual coming together of various strands of knowledge and skill. There is the story of the child's journey from scribble to script, from letter strings to real words, and from short, simple messages to messages that are reasonably detailed and somewhat coherent. This book also describes the setting—the time, places, materials, and people that must be available to assist children in their journey, if this story is to end as we would hope— with competent children, full of ideas, eager to record their ideas, and confident in their ability to write.

CHAPTER 2

From Scribble to Script

This chapter chronicles the development of marks children use for writing, from children's first intentional use of lines for the purpose of writing to the point at which they exert a fair measure of control over the form of their written marks. The development we consider here typically spans from 2 or $2^1/_2$ years of age to a little over 5 years of age—from the late toddler stage through the end of the preschool years (Baghban, 1984; Clay, 1987; Schickedanz, 1990).

The First Discovery: "I Can Make Marks"

The young child's world is full of designs on paper and on a variety of other surfaces. Writing materials and the visual aspects of writing and drawing fascinate young children. The child's discovery that writing and drawing tools leave tracks, and that the form of these is under the child's control, sparks curiosity. The child moves the tool in one way and looks. The child moves it in a different way and looks. The child moves the tool in a flurry, back and forth, round and round, jab, jab, jab. And looks. To anyone watching, it appears that the child is thinking, "How do I make the design I want? What did I do to get that design?"

For several months, the toddler experiments and seems happy with his or her actions, whatever the results. Then, a new question seems to occur to the exploring child: "How do I re-create a certain effect, the design I want? What is the action that results in a *specific* effect?" This question emerges as marks produced in free exploration begin to remind the child of something. Consider the drawing in Figure 2, which was created by a 2-year-old who was exploring with a marker on white notepaper. The child was silent, absorbed in the doing, until he finished drawing. He looked a long time at this drawing, touched it several times, and then said, "A man." Then, he pointed to the two spots in the top portion and said, "Eyes," and then to the large inside circle in the middle and said, "Mouth."

It is doubtful that the child intended to create any specific design when he first put pen to paper, but suddenly, there it was—a happy accident, the

Figure 2
A Child's Free Exploration Drawing: "A Man"

result of a series of random, exploratory movements. With new interest in the marks, the child began to wonder, "I want to do that again, but how? What did I do to produce this result?"

Marking becomes more deliberate after this question comes to the child's mind. Of course, not every occasion of marking is guided by such thoughts; at first, the thought isn't there very much of the time. The sheer joy of creating marks dominates the child's marking for many months, and it remains a motivation for writing throughout the early childhood years. The difference now is that there are moments, and an ever-increasing number of them, when action is deliberate. The child wants to make a line look a certain way, or to create a particular form that represents a specific image.

Or the child wants to make it clear that marks made on a specific occasion are not a picture of something, but "say something." Marking and meaning become joined on these occasions of deliberate action. The child uses marks—tries to control marks—to serve his or her representational purposes.

This Is Writing, Not a Picture

If someone were to show you the four samples in Figure 3, odds are you would know at a glance that Figure 3a is writing. Figure 3b, on the other hand, might require some study: Is it the result of a child's random exploration with a marker, or a picture of something, such as a face with bangs covering the forehead, or a bowl of spaghetti with a noodle hanging over the edge? As it turns out, Figure 3b is a phone message, written by a 3-year-old in the **dramatic play** area of her preschool classroom. The marks in the other two samples in Figure 3 also are writing; both are children's signatures. One (3c) was used to label a block building; the other (3d) was written on the back of the child's paper collage. All of these scribble samples were created by children who were between $2\frac{1}{2}$ and $3\frac{1}{2}$ years of age.

These representations are typical of children who are at the very beginning of their journey into learning how to mark meanings. Here, in this first step, we see no difference between the marks the child uses to draw pictures and those that are intended to "say something." We know the child's intention only by listening or by watching the context in which the child applies the marking tool to paper.

But soon, almost on the heels of the dawning of representational intentions, we see evidence that the child has made an important distinction. The child understands that marks used for writing look different from those used for drawing pictures. Figures 4a and 4b on page 14 illustrate this insight. We can see that scribble marks were used to create both a picture and some writing. The child drew a picture in the middle of the paper and then placed writing at the bottom of the page. The writing represented the following message: "Dear Mommy, I love you. Dear Daddy, I love you too. And my name."

Notice that the writing is lined up and the lines are isolated from one another. The child exerts more control over the marks intended as writing; they are not allowed to go all over. The internal variations in the lines of writing are also reasonably uniform, as if the child has noticed that the same details repeat frequently in a way that details do not typically repeat in a picture. In the picture, on the other hand, lines meander and intertwine, as if each can be allowed to have a mind of its own. As a result, the

Figure 3
Is It a Picture, or Is It Writing?

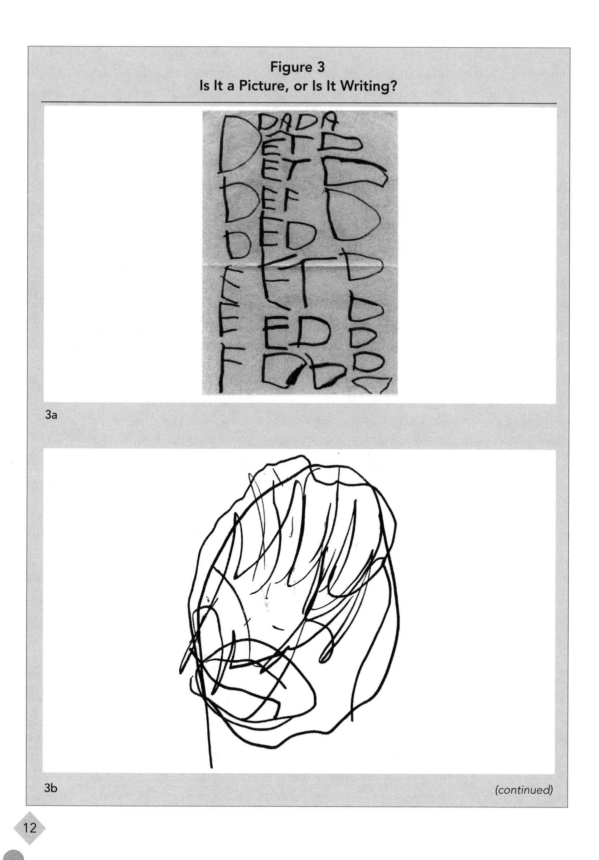

3a

3b

(continued)

Figure 3 (continued)

3c

3d

Figure 4
Writing Marks Are Lined Up, Picture Marks Are Not

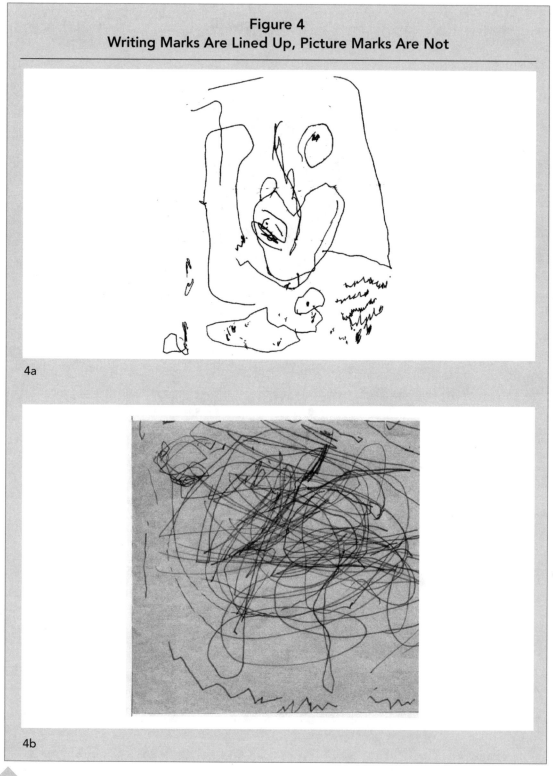

4a

4b

picture contains greater variation in form than we see in the writing. Clearly, the child who created this sample is aware of two general worlds of marks—a world of pictures and a world of print. This is another major discovery for the young child.

Details, Details: Increasing Focus on the Features of Print Symbols

In the world of print, individual lines and designs—alphabet letters—make up the lines that children perceive. At first, the line itself, the fact of a linear arrangement, is all that registers with the child. This linear arrangement is what makes a collection of marks serve as writing and not as a picture. As was noted earlier, children indicate even in their first scribbles that they perceive some degree of detail within lines of print, but they represent this perception only with zigs and zags of various densities. In Figure 4a the zigs and zags are quite dense, but there is little variation in the details included to compose the line. Most "details" look very much alike, although the peaks and valleys of the zigs and zags do vary a bit, as does the distance between them.

The scribble lines making up the letter shown in Figure 5a have even less of this kind of variation than the scribble writing in Figure 4. In contrast, the lines in Figure 5b, which were created by a young 4-year-old who was playing at producing writing, have very dense zigs and zags that vary considerably from one another. And, yet, the child is still using *only* zigs and zags.

When we compare 5b with 5c and 5d, we notice something new in the last two. The marks that make up the line of print in 5c contain a few zigs and zags but also some loops. The first line even starts with a separate small form, a closed curve or circle. There are a few other marks that stand alone, such as the small closed curve with a tail at the beginning of line four, and the small vertical line at the beginning of line five. In line four, we also can see that the child started with a zigzag that looks very much like *W*, and then followed it, not with another zigzag, but with a closed curve (similar to *O*). This closed curve is followed by another zigzag line, but it is open at the bottom rather than at the top, which looks like *M*. This detail is followed by another closed loop, but this one is oriented differently and lacks the symmetry of the closed curve that the child placed earlier in the line. This kind of variation in the forms included in a line indicates that the

Figure 5
Scribble Writing and Looped Mock Letters

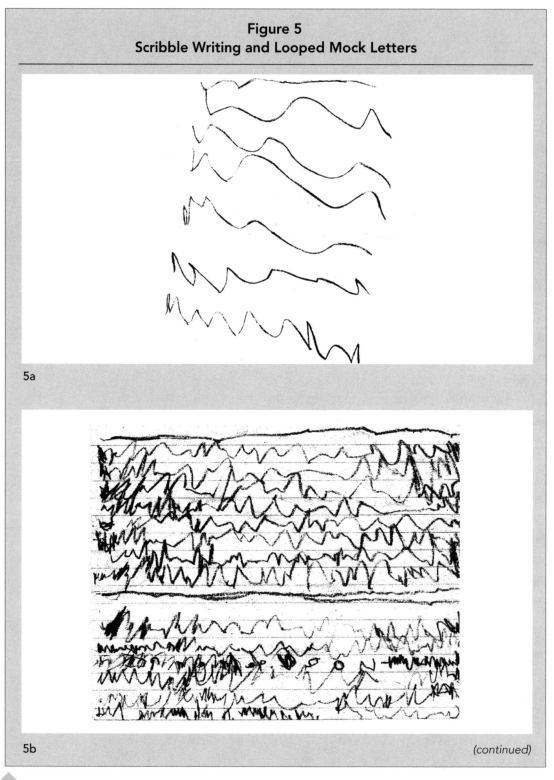

5a

5b

(continued)

Figure 5 (continued)

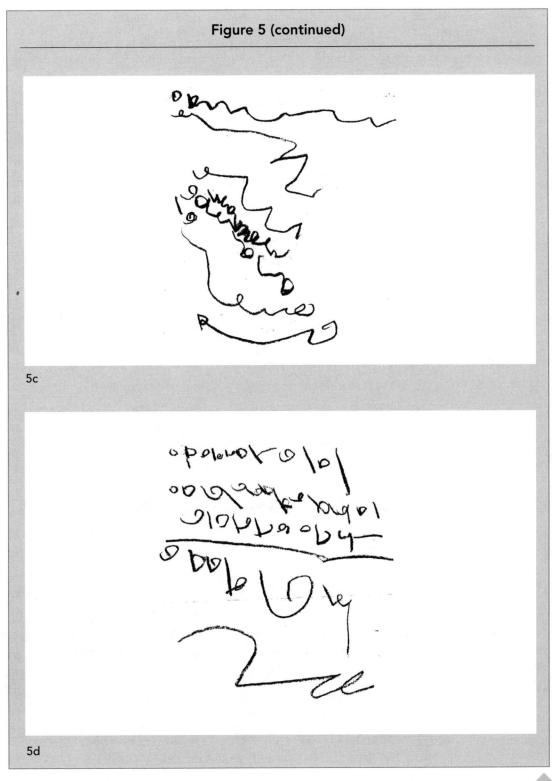

5c

5d

child is aware of the different shapes of symbols that make up the words in a line of print.

Figure 5d was created by the same 4-year-old who created 5c. She turned over her paper to write "a letter." But here, she used almost no scribble writing. For the most part, these marks are **mock letters**, and they seem to have been influenced considerably by cursive writing, which this child observed in the adult writing around her. The letters *a*, *c*, and *e* appeared in her name, and adults in her family wrote these for her in lowercase (as none of these letters was the first letter in her name). The noncurved lines in her name were *t* and *y*. We can see the influence of all these letters in the child's writing, although she took some liberties as well. When writing her letter, she created some new forms that are not found in the English alphabet. The children who created the samples shown in Figure 6 also created new forms.

Figure 6a is a 4-year-old's grocery list. We see some lines of scribble, but among the scribbles are distinct little forms, some of which are mock letters. In 6b there are many mock letters and a few actual letters (*A*, *R*, *V*, and *O*). In Figure 6c, we see many actual letters and a few mock letters, especially those that resemble long *E*'s with extra horizontal lines. We also see what appear to be upside-down *T*'s, plus a few long vertical lines with a closed circle placed in the middle of their lower ends, not to one side or the other as in actual letters, such as *b* and *d*.

Mock letters, which display many characteristics of alphabet letters, contain the segments that are the building blocks of actual letters. To understand what is probably going on in the child's mind, let's consider Legos, Tinker Toys, and wooden blocks—three popular construction toys. These toys are packaged with an insert that shows a few specific items that can be made with the materials provided. Of course, the possibilities are vast and the child invents many original designs. But no matter what a child builds, the basic materials make all the structures created with a particular construction toy look like they belong together. They are of the same kind, because the basic pieces used to make each item come from the same set of materials.

It's the same with creating letters. A limited set of lines is available to make all letters of the alphabet. Some lines are used in some letters; other lines are used in other letters. Often the same kinds of lines are used in many letters, but their number varies (compare *E* and *F*), as does the placement

Figure 6
From Mock Letters to Real Letters

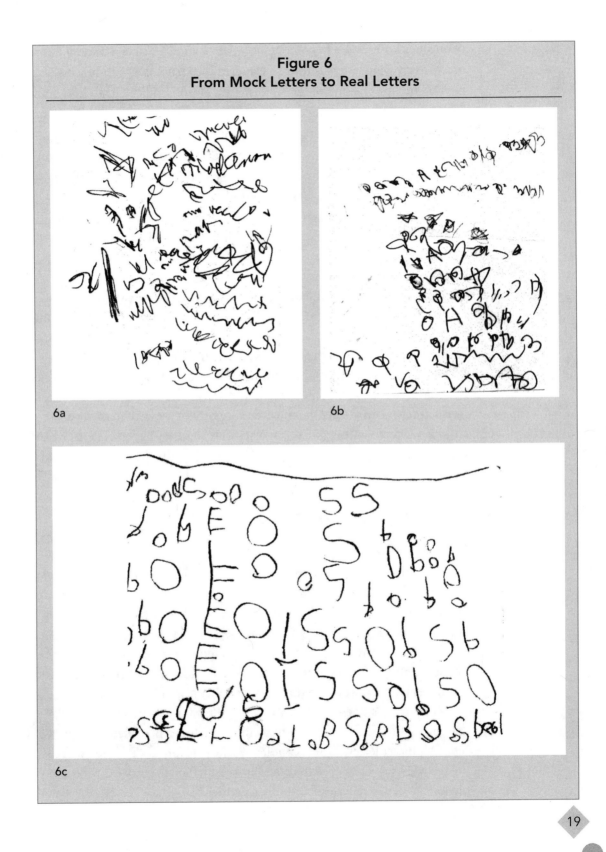

6a

6b

6c

of one line with respect to another (compare *d* and *b*). There is a second way in which creating letters is the same as creating structures with blocks: The possibilities for creating different forms are almost endless. The child does not yet know that there are only 26 letters, and that all the possibilities for creating forms with this set of lines are not exploited in creating our alphabet. For all the child knows, there could be 50 or 100 letters, just as there are endless possibilities for different constructions, given the same set of blocks, or the same pieces of a Tinker Toys set.

Under these circumstances, why wouldn't a child combine lines in any way possible? The child might very well think, "Surely this is a letter, although perhaps I haven't actually seen one like this before." Until a child has had several years of experience, including exposure to a variety of alphabet puzzles, alphabet books, and words in the environment, we are likely to see mock letters in his or her writing. When a child builds with construction toys, teachers praise creativity and encourage unique constructions. But with writing, the rules change—socialization narrows the possibilities. Eventually, the almost infinite number of possible marks is winnowed out to a standard set. During the preschool years, as children devise new letter forms, teachers must tolerate, and even support, their creativity. After all, the child is working within the set of lines that we use to produce letters. In time, and rather quickly actually, children narrow the designs of their creations so that even mock letters look very much like actual letters.

Children Realize There Is a Limited Set of Letters

One day, after finishing an alphabet puzzle, a child who was almost 5 years old asked his teacher, "Are these all the alphabet letters in the whole wide world?" She asked what made him think that this might be all of them. "Because," he said, "I see the same ones everywhere!" The teacher explained that the puzzle the child had just completed did indeed contain all the English alphabet letters in the whole wide world, but that there are other languages in the world with different alphabet symbols.

This child's question reveals an insight: Everywhere we look, we see the same letters. In time, the young child concludes that there is a limited set of alphabet letters, not an endless variety of forms. "People don't approach the set of lines used to create alphabet letters the way I approach my blocks," a child concludes, "and I won't either."

Creating Scribbles, Mock Letters, and Actual Letters

Once children have attained the insight that there are just a few letters, not an endless number, mock letters seldom appear in their writing, except perhaps during dramatic play, where it is sometimes necessary to generate a lot of writing in a short amount of time. When children make props for play scenarios, they generally recognize that the props are "just pretend" and that written marks needn't be "real" letters. Writing for this purpose, even among 5-year-olds, may be a combination of scribbles, mock letters, and actual letters. More often, though, we see actual letters, or good approximations to them, combined with scribble writing. Scribble writing is easier and faster to produce than are mock or actual letters. We see just this combination of marks on a ticket a child prepared for a classroom production of *The Three Little Pigs* (see Figure 7). Notice that the forms at the top of the ticket are the numerals 1 through 10.

In nonplay situations, the older 4-year-old and younger 5-year-old typically use forms that are actual letters, although their skill in creating them is limited in many ways. Consider the samples provided in Figure 8.

Figure 8a comes from a sign-up sheet provided in a block area. When the block area was full (occupants were limited to four at a time), children who wanted turns wrote their names on a sheet of paper attached to a clipboard. The name at the top of this list is *SARAH*. The child started in the middle of the paper with *S*, wrote *A* and *R*, and then ran out of room.

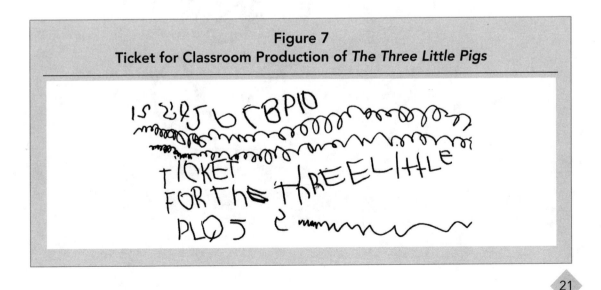

Figure 7
Ticket for Classroom Production of *The Three Little Pigs*

Figure 8
Where to Start, and Where to Go?

8a

8b

She returned to the middle of the paper, and wrote *A* to the left of *S*, and *H* to the left of that. Budding knowledge of **directionality** collides with the challenges of specific situations.

Sarah's print placement strategies are very typical among preschoolers. She started in a place that did not give her enough space to write all of a word on one line. Then she fit in the rest of the letters as best she could. Sometimes, children turn the paper and write the remaining letters on what had been the right side of the paper, but ends up, at least for a time, as the top.

Notice that Sarah knew the letters of her name, wrote them in the correct order, and started out writing from left to right. Had Sarah started at the left-hand margin (rather than in the middle of the page), she might have returned to the left to finish writing. But there was space, right there on the original line, so why not fill it?

Had a teacher not seen Sarah write her name, she might have drawn the conclusion that Sarah started with *H* and went from there, jumbling the order of the letters. Not so. Sarah did not yet know that she should *always* sweep to the left and write the remaining letters from left to right under her top row. Such a strategy might actually seem very inefficient to a young child in Sarah's situation: "Why waste all that space I left on the first line?" "Why separate my name by putting letters on two different lines?"

Thinking of this kind was exactly what made a different child resist her teacher's suggestion that she put the *A* that follows *R* in the word *library* under the *L* she had written in the first line (see Figure 8b). She wanted the *R* and *A* to be "together," she explained, "because they come together in the word." Children have their reasons for doing things. Gradually, they begin to see things as adults see them. In the meantime, we can enjoy their efforts and accept some of their thoughtful accommodations to challenges they encounter when putting print on a page.

A Close Look at the Letters Preschoolers Create

Preschoolers also form letters in interesting ways. Notice that Sarah reversed the *S* in her name. *S* is a difficult letter for young children to orient correctly. Make the first move in the wrong direction and the letter is reversed. Notice that the only other curved line in Sarah's name is in the upper portion of *R* and that the movement for the curved line in this letter starts in the opposite direction. Children must build motor habits (routine ways of moving) for specific letters, and this takes time. Reversed letters are very common in the writing of preschool and kindergarten children. In most cases, there is no confusion about which letter they have written, and it must seem to preschoolers that orientation should not matter. However, orientation does matter. Teachers support children's acquisition of knowledge about letter orientation when they comment that "*M* and *W* are just alike, except one faces up and the other faces down." For older preschoolers, teachers might contrast the direction of movement when making *S* and *2* in quick demonstrations provided at the writing table. When writing an experience chart with a group of children, a teacher might comment, when starting the letter *S*, "I start here and then go this way, and then back around like this. If I go the other way, my *S* will be backward."

We also see a lot of imprecision in the marks the children used to compose the letters. Notice the *B* in *LIBRARY* in Figure 8b. The child did splendidly with the top closed curve but had some difficulty with the bottom portion. (Did she think *P* at first, and then repair it to form a *B*? We don't know.) The *R*'s in *LIBRARY* are also interesting. The diagonal line that makes up the lower right half of *R* gave the child some trouble. Diagonal lines are difficult, as we will see again in some later samples. Sarah's *H* and one *A* are also interesting. In the *H*, the horizontal bar is placed about as low as it can go on the right side. But notice the tiny bit of the right vertical line that extends below it. The *A* between the *H* and the *S* also is pushing the limits a bit. *A*'s are closed at the top, not open. When open, they begin to pass into *H* territory. But Sarah uses straight lines for *H* and diagonal lines for *A*, and there's no confusion between these two letters in her writing. Besides, there's just a small gap in the top of that *A*, nothing serious.

We see some of the same difficulties and a few others in the samples in Figure 9. All these samples are color names devised by children for a class book on colors.

Figure 9a says, "Zebra black." Notice the difficulty with diagonal lines in both *Z* and *k*. Notice how well formed the other letters are, and that they are in lowercase as well, except for the second *A* (the one in the middle of *black*). We can see the struggle the child had with the lowercase *a* at the end of *Zebra*. Perhaps the child did not want to attempt another one.

This is how it is with preschoolers. There is tentative trying of the new, and then a return to the familiar, especially with such important writing to do. Teachers model both uppercase and lowercase letters in their own writing, and children gain further exposure to both kinds of letters

Figure 9
Typical Errors in Preschoolers' Letter Formation

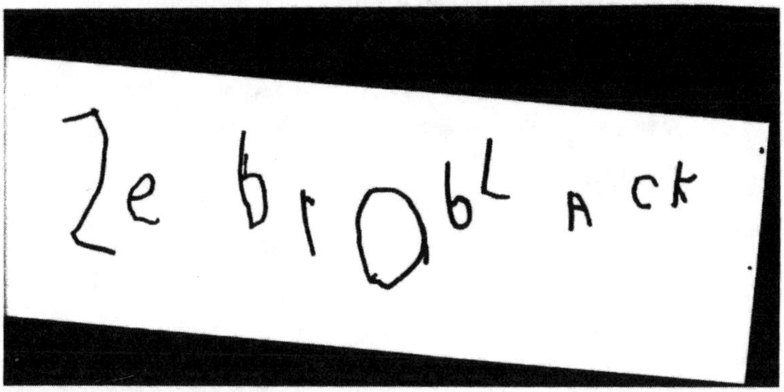

9a

9b

9c

through environmental print and books. Slowly, they give it a try. We shouldn't worry in the preschool years about where children use lower-case and uppercase. Knowing that there are two kinds of letters, big and little ones, and familiarity with how each looks is plenty for children to know in these early years.

Figure 9b (*BLUE BERRY*) was also created by a child for the class color book. Look at the *E*'s. The first horizontal line does not start right at the top of the vertical left post, and the horizontal lines are larger than usual. The curved lines at the top of both the *B*'s and *R*'s also don't start at the top. What was the child thinking? We don't know, but it doesn't matter because we know what letters the child intended.

Figure 9c (*CHERRY*) was created by a third child. Notice the fancy *E*. Mock letter *E*'s of this kind are almost universal in children's writing. Children add lines in an apparent attempt to amplify the letter *E*. Perhaps they think there is more "E-ness" this way. They have a good point, and there is no confusion between this *E* and any other letter in the word. All children stop doing this, in time. It's nothing to worry about.

Notice the struggle here with the diagonal line for the right side of the *R*. This is a common challenge for all preschoolers, as we have already seen. The *C* in this sample is also interesting, given that it was formed out of three lines—first a vertical one at the left, and then two other short ones, one at the top and one at the bottom. These color names were written on strips of paper. How does a child make sure she doesn't go over the left edge of the strip, especially with a curved line that takes a good bit of control? A child might think, "Don't even attempt it. Make the *C* in a different way that I can control better." Children are always thinking.

Why Preschoolers Write the Way They Write

Some of the imprecision we see in young children's letter formation is cognitive. Preschool children seem to judge whether the marks they make will be interpreted as intended or will be confused with another letter. Had Sarah thought there was any question about the *A* she had formed in writing her name on the sign-up sheet (see Figure 8a), she might have used another mark to connect the top of her *A*. Children do that all the time—they go back and tidy up their work.

The problem of diagonal lines is cognitive. "Where do I start?" "Where do I aim?" It's a projective space problem. The child must imagine the line needed, before starting. Adults often think that children can easily transfer mental images of alphabet letters onto paper. Children certainly work from an image, but re-creating these images on paper—in two-dimensional space—is not easy. Even a physical model to copy does not help. The line in the copy is there, already formed. The child might wonder, "How did someone *do* that?" "How do I move my marker to re-create that shape?" If a young child wants help, an adult can draw the letter on another piece of paper, while describing each move he or she makes. Then, the adult can draw it again, line segment by line segment, while the child does the same segments on his or her paper, after the teacher draws his or her own. Then, for a diagonal line, such as in *R* or *K*, the teacher can place strategic dots. For *R*, place one dot on the vertical line where the child starts, and the other at the stopping point. For *K*, place one dot where the child starts and another at the midpoint of the vertical line.

Formal handwriting lessons do not belong in the preschool, but explicit instruction can be given in response to a child's requests. Preschoolers often make such requests, over time, as they strive to get their representations of specific letters to look the way these letters look everywhere else they see them. "I can't do *R*," they say. Or someone announces, "My *S* is going the wrong way again. Help me!"

Some of the young child's difficulty in forming letters is not cognitive but stems from immature fine-motor skills. When the marking tool is held in a rigid fist grip and the movement comes from the muscle of the upper arm, it's difficult, if not impossible, to create and combine lines with precision. It's still difficult to be precise when the writing tool is held rigidly in the fingers and the movement comes by moving the entire hand at the wrist. Thus, preschoolers write big letters, and often their letters have a lot of line overruns. Notice the *H*, *A*'s, and *R* in Sarah's name (see Figure 8a). Lines that meet do not stop at the meeting point. They go beyond. Look at the *A* in *LIBRARY* and you will see the same thing (see Figure 8b).

We see no overruns in Figure 9a. This child had exceptional fine-motor skill for a preschooler, which explains not only the absence of major line overruns, but probably the use of so many lowercase letters. Lowercase letters are more difficult to form than are uppercase letters, and they require considerably more finger dexterity.

We do see line overrun in Figure 9b, although it's not a big problem. This is not careless or sloppy writing. This is wonderful writing, given the typical preschool child's level of motor control. It's rather amazing how hard preschoolers try to keep their writing within reasonable bounds, despite their motor limitations. They try to avoid overlapping and over-running lines, even though precision of movement is difficult for them.

Summary

The preschool years are remarkable years for learning and development. As we have seen in this chapter, a young child's writing evolves from scribble to script in a matter of only two or three years. To be sure, the child still has much to learn. But any child who travels the distance described here is off to a wonderful start.

The preschool teacher and the child's family have a front row seat for observing these remarkable achievements. And, in many important ways, they also set the stage for the opportunities a child has to write, and for providing the support children need along the way. We will consider ways of providing support for children's writing in chapter 5.

CHAPTER 3

From Letter Strings to Real Words

W e discussed in chapter 2 how the marks children use for writing gradually change from scribble to **mock letters** and reasonable approximations of conventional forms. As preschool children continue to develop their skill in forming letters, they also begin to learn how to use letters to create words.

Throughout the preschool years, children make considerable progress in developing a beginning understanding of word making. In kindergarten and beyond, they continue to acquire the knowledge and skills (including spelling skills) required for conventional word making. Children very slowly begin to grasp the pivotal importance of the selection and sequencing of print symbols in written communication as they observe and interact with the print that surrounds them, as they talk about their writing with their teachers, and as their teachers provide demonstrations of writing and activities that foster children's **phonological awareness** and letter-name knowledge.

At first, preschoolers have no understanding that print is mapped onto **oral language**. They experiment freely with ways of using letters to create words. Even after children acquire the basic insight that print and speech are related, the precise way in which they are related eludes them. Only gradually do preschoolers begin to realize that letters represent the individual sounds in spoken words. Isolating sounds and knowing which letters are used to represent them are skills beyond the capability of most preschoolers. Yet, we do see the beginnings of conventional word making, even in these early years. This chapter examines the development of children's understanding about how letters are used to make words and offers teachers suggestions for supporting children's learning. It is based on the systematic work by Baghban (1984), Clay (1975), and Invernizzi (2003), and on the countless contributions of others who have studied young children's writing.

Children's Names as Sources of Knowledge About Word Making

As we see in Figure 10, pictures and letter shapes are often equally prominent in a child's earliest attempts to use letters to convey specific meanings. This sample was produced by 3-year-old Brianna in a post office dramatic play center. Together, the pictures and letters constituted a letter to her aunt. When her teacher asked what the letter said, Brianna read, "Dear Auntie Shante, I am coming to see you. Me and Mommy and Henry. We coming. Love, Brianna."

Figure 10
Brianna's Letter

"Dear Auntie Shante, I am coming to see you. Me and Mommy and Henry. We coming. Love, Brianna."

For Brianna, meaning was conveyed as much by the picture as by the print. She relied on oral language to explain both pictures and letters. The important thing to know about the letters, though, was that almost all were from her name. She indicated that the *NA* at the bottom of the page said *love Brianna*. Apparently, Brianna knew that letters were needed to write the rest of her message to her aunt, so she borrowed some from her name. The understanding that we can write our name and then use the same letters again to write additional words is rare among young 3-year-olds. The letters in their name are "theirs" and every word they see with a letter from their name in it is likely to be claimed as "mine." Brianna's writing demonstrates a budding understanding that letters in her name also can be used for other words. But she seems to have thought to herself, "Not at the same time!"

As described in an earlier chapter, and as we have just seen in Brianna's letter, the first letters to appear in children's writing are typically those found in words that are most familiar to them—especially their names. At age 3, Billy, a classmate of Brianna, had shown a lot of interest in his name. He could spell it aloud, letter by letter, and he tried to write it, too, although he wasn't always able to write each letter as he spelled it. Billy wrote a letter to his older brother, Odell, who had gone on a trip with their father. Figure 11 shows that Billy used variations of his name over and over again to complete his letter. He read it to his teacher as follows: "Odell, I been missing you. Come home tomorrow. Love, Billy. Come home now."

Figure 11
Billy's Letter

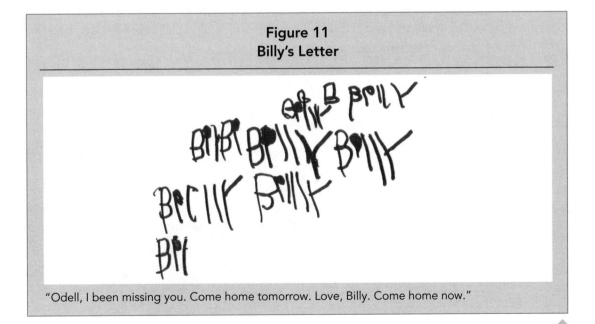

"Odell, I been missing you. Come home tomorrow. Love, Billy. Come home now."

While still relying on his name as his basic source of letters to write his message to his brother, Billy nonetheless demonstrated a more sophisticated understanding of writing than did Brianna. He reused letters in his name, and altered the sequence that is found in his name, to create other "words." Apparently, he had observed that the same letters can be used to spell many different words and that some words differ by only one letter (e.g., *cake* and *Coke*; *Mike* and *Ike*). Notice that in many cases Billy added just one new mark to *Billy* (e.g., *Billly*, *BiClly*, and *Belly*). In the case of *Belly*, the addition of a letter *e* substituted for the letter that occupies that spot in his name (*i*). In one "word," Billy used a second strategy—he recombined letters to create a new sequence (*BilBi*). He also used a third strategy—deletion of letters so that a shorter "word" (*Bil*) was created.

Random Use of Environmental Print

As children gain more experience with words such as their names and the names of classmates, they begin to pay increasing attention to the print they see around them. The more print-rich their environment, the more opportunities they have to become aware of letters beyond those in their own names and to observe that the same letters can be combined in many different sequences to create different words (Fields, 1998; Invernizzi, 2003). This awareness of environmental print frequently leads children to produce writing that is composed of nonsense words. These strings of letters mimic the look of real words. They are **mock words**—arrangements of letters that closely follow the *look* of actual words, even though they do not represent real words in our language.

In this phase of writing with letters, children have not yet discovered that letters used must be connected to the sequence of sounds in the words of a message. We say that children lack an understanding of the **alphabetic principle**. They do not understand that letters represent sounds. Their intention is to make their writing look like it is composed of words, and they do accomplish that.

The writing sample in Figure 12 was produced by 5-year-old Marisol at the **writing center** in her preschool classroom. According to Marisol, her writing says, "I like my dog. I take good care of him." Her writing, like Billy's, uses **nonphonemic letter strings**—letters selected and sequenced without regard to the sound structure of the word—and is typical of children who do not yet have any idea that speech sounds and letters are connected, or any inkling of the level of sound (i.e., individual phonemes) that

Figure 12
Marisol's Writing

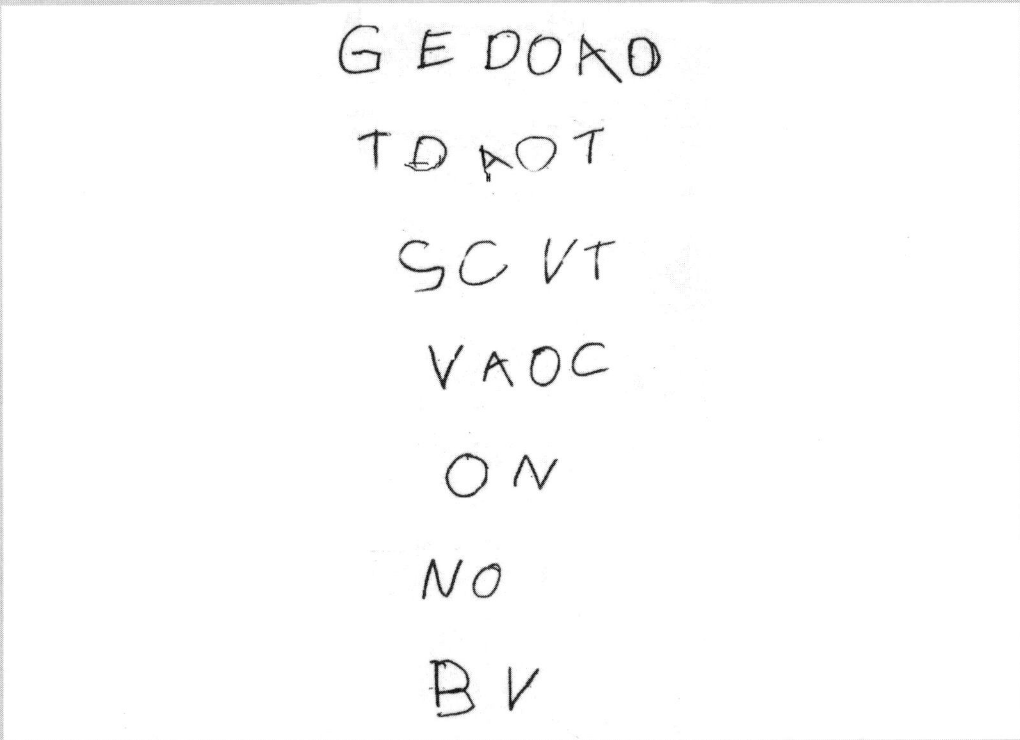

GE DOAO

TD AOT

SC VT

VAOC

O N

NO

B V

"I like my dog. I take good care of him."

letters code. Unlike Billy, Marisol uses many letters, not just those drawn mostly from her name. In fact, there are 11 distinct letters among the 25 letters she created in this sample. Her writing looks a lot more like "real" writing than Billy's because she has written many more words, even though these are mock words, just as Billy's were.

Although the variations in her mock words make it look like Marisol knows a lot more about word making than Billy does, the two children follow the same basic strategy of combining letters so that they look like a word. However, we get the impression that Marisol has carefully inspected a wider range of real words than has Billy, and that she knows many more alphabet letters. This additional knowledge, and perhaps her more frequent engagement with print in the environment beyond her own name, will inform her word-making knowledge and may help her move ahead more quickly than Billy in attempting to write words using a sound-based strategy.

Like Billy and Marisol, Jeffrey wrote nonphonemic letter strings (see Figure 13). As read to his teacher, his composition says, "My mom and dad like to play. They like to play with my sisters and my dog, too." Note that Jeffrey attempted to make his writing appear more conventional by adding periods at the end of each line of print. This detail suggests that he has attended to the print in his environment and has noticed some written marks that are not alphabet letters. Sometimes, children even draw lines under their mock words, apparently because they have seen a lot of writing positioned on lines and they think that these marks are somehow essential for "real" writing. Children pay close attention to the print they see and they try to incorporate visual elements that make their efforts resemble the real thing.

Figure 13
Jeffrey's Composition

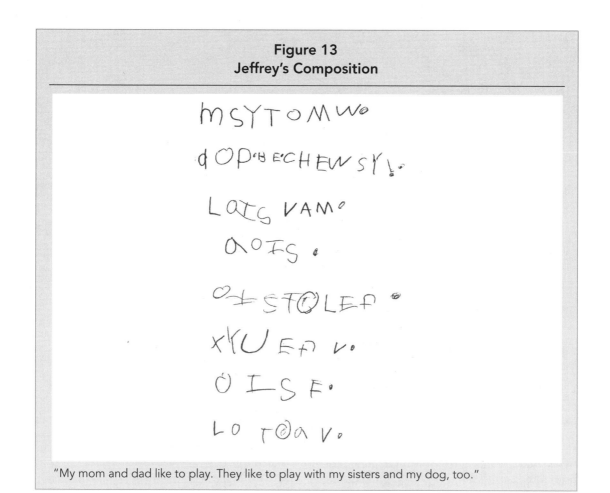

"My mom and dad like to play. They like to play with my sisters and my dog, too."

Beginnings of Phonemic Spelling

A major developmental leap in writing occurs when children discover that the selection and sequence of letters in a word have some connection to the word's sounds. A beginning awareness of the sounds in words, called **phonological awareness**, begins long before children display any awareness of sound–print links in their writing. Young children first demonstrate phonological awareness as they begin to recognize or produce rhyming words and as they orally divide syllables into onsets (first sounds) and rimes (the remaining sounds in syllables). This level of phonological processing precedes more sophisticated **phonemic awareness**, which develops gradually as children become increasingly able to distinguish each of the discrete sounds in spoken words.

During the preschool years, beginning levels of phonological awareness develop as children engage in language play involving rhyme and alliteration. Children's phonemic-level awareness can be enhanced when teachers call children's attention to the individual sounds in oral language (Invernizzi, 2003). For example, singing songs that manipulate sounds in words provides wonderful experience of this kind. Consider "Apples and Bananas," a song by Raffi: "I like to eat, eat, eat, apples and bananas…I like to eat, eat, eat, eeples an beeneenees…I like to ote, ote, ote, opels and bononoes…" (Raffi, 1985). As children sing this song and others (e.g., "Willoughby Wallaby Woo"), they experience the changing of some individual sounds in words while holding others constant. Such experiences scaffold children's learning by providing a level of support that enables successful manipulation of sounds. In this case, the song itself provides the support children require by leading them to play with sounds, even though they might not be skilled in isolating and manipulating phonemes on their own. Over time, repeated engagement in this type of playful activity leads to growth in phonological awareness.

Preschool teachers may also enhance children's awareness of the individual sounds in speech by reciting poems and playing games like "I Spy," in which children are encouraged to find objects in the classroom that begin with particular sounds. For example, a teacher might say, "I spy something that starts with /m/, like Marisol's name…/m/ *Marisol*. I want you to think about objects in our classroom and think about whether any of them have names that start with /m/." To participate, children must say the names of objects they see or know about and then isolate the first sound of an object's name. They must then match it to /m/, the target sound the teacher has provided. As you can see, this activity requires children to isolate the individual sound—the phoneme—at the beginning of a word.

Numerous learning-center activities that engage children in sorting small items or pictures according to their beginning sounds will further develop children's phonemic awareness. Learning-center activities should be introduced and modeled in a large-group, teacher-directed setting. This instruction and practice provide children with the background they need to successfully use the materials in an independent learning center. All these activities—songs, teacher-directed instruction and practice games, and follow-up learning-center activities—help children attend to the first sounds in words and also develop children's ability to manipulate sounds in words.

While phonemic awareness is important for phonemic-based writing (e.g., *KT* instead of *TPAS* for *CAT*), it is not sufficient. Children also need to connect letters to sounds they hear. To do this, they must distinguish among letter shapes and know each letter's name. They then need to know that letters are used to write sounds we hear in words. This insight is known as the alphabetic principle. If children do not understand how letters function in words, they will not use letters systematically in their writing. Many young children can recognize and name all the letters of the alphabet but have no idea how to use them to make words. The teacher must provide demonstrations that help children realize that individual sounds they hear in words are written with specific letters.

Teachers can help children make these connections by sounding out words as they demonstrate writing. This thinking aloud, as the teacher writes, can be done as a natural part of preschool classroom routines. A teacher may, for example, involve the children in making signs to label art-center supplies. She might say, "This sign is for the markers. Let's see, /m/, /m/, /m/, /m/…*markers*. The word *markers* starts with the letter *m*, so I'll write the *m* first, right here." The teacher might then say, "I hear /r/ next, but I know there's an *a* before it that we don't hear, so I will write that first and then write *r* for /r/. Then, I hear /k/, mark /k/, and we use *k* to write /k/, so I'll write *k* next…." By transcribing a spoken message into its written form, the teacher explicitly models the most fundamental literacy concept—the fact that print conveys meaning. Such an authentic use of print will serve many important literacy purposes and also serves the social purpose of helping to keep the art center neat.

Another activity that should be used routinely in the preschool classroom is labeling children's drawings or paintings as the children dictate the words. Again, the teacher can think aloud the spelling of some of the most prominent words as they are written. A teacher has yet another opportunity when a child "anchors" a message in scribble writing and then approaches the teacher to talk about it. If the child is agreeable, and if it serves the child's purposes, the teacher can help in writing some actual words to go with the scribble the child has created. Perhaps the child would like the teacher to write "Dear Mommy" or some other part of the message. The teacher can use the highly informative think-aloud strategy when helping the child.

When children begin to understand the connection between sounds and letters, they often begin to create very primitive phonemic spellings on their own. Sometimes, this occurs while they are still writing letters that are not very conventional. Figure 14 demonstrates Elizabeth's budding awareness of sound–letter connections. She created this message for a class-mate's birthday. She explained to her teacher that it says, "Happy Birthday, Maria. She's 4. Happy Birthday."

Figure 14
Elizabeth's Birthday Greeting

"Happy Birthday, Maria. She's 4. Happy Birthday."

While the somewhat haphazard placement of the letters on the page makes it seem as if they might have been selected at random, it is quite likely that Elizabeth selected the letters *H* and *P* because she detected the initial and middle consonant sounds in *happy* and matched these sounds to these two letters. Of course, Elizabeth might have seen *Happy Birthday* written somewhere and simply remembered the first letter and a middle letter in the first word. We cannot know for sure. But just this sort of word spelling (*HP* for *happy*) begins to appear once children try to sound out words for themselves.

Elizabeth's use of just a few letters to stand for a whole word is typical of children who first begin to use phonemic spelling. It is common for young writers to represent syllables or entire words with single letters. *HP* for *happy* is an interesting example of such abbreviated word making. First, the second phoneme in *happy* is a soft vowel, which is relatively hard to hear. Second, there is only one phoneme in the middle of *happy*, despite the fact that the word is conventionally spelled with two *p*'s. Finally, the name of *P* has two phonemes, /p/ and /ē/; these phonemes are found in the same order in *happy*. When writing a word that contains the same phonemes as a letter name, sometimes the child will use that letter in a "two for one" way. It seems likely that Elizabeth chose *P* to represent both /p/ and /ē/. In summary, Elizabeth did a great job of coding the sounds in this word. She missed only one sound—the second—the one that is very hard to hear.

Children's growing awareness of phonemic spelling does not necessarily lead them immediately to abandon earlier forms of word making. Figure 15 illustrates the extent to which children mix forms. Five-year-old Jackson read this journal entry as, "My mom fixes me spinach and turkey and gravy. It is good." This appears at first glance to be a mix of non-phonemic letter strings and scribble writing. Closer examination, however, reveals that Jackson engaged in significant phonemic spelling. The *mi* on the first line may represent *my*, while the *fes* is for *fixes*. The word *me* is represented with a single letter *m*, and *spinach* is spelled *snh*, representing the three major consonant sounds he hears. The letter strings and scribble that follow the first two lines suggest that Jackson wanted to create lots of writing but couldn't sustain the level of effort needed to continue sounding out words and selecting letters.

Jackson's choice of the letter *H* to represent /ch/ in *spinach* is an interesting example of the letter-name spelling strategy used by many preschoolers when they first link letters to sounds they have isolated. When children isolate a sound in a word they want to spell, they use the letter that

Figure 15
Jackson's Journal Entry

M iniefEsms n H

Nren gre

O p r m HfGI

O IS r30 00 +

cwueusu

"My mom fixes me spinach and turkey and gravy. It is good."

has this sound in its name. In the case of /ch/ as in *chip* or *chair*, there is a letter name that is a correct match. The second sound in the name of the letter *H* (aich) is this very sound.

This strategy is also evident in children's use of single letters to represent entire words, as when they write *C* for *see*, *R* for *are*, and *U* for *you*. In these cases, the letter names have in them the sequence of two sounds heard in these words.

Later Movement Along a Developmental Continuum

Once children fully understand that writing involves organizing letters into clusters based on the sound sequence in words, they follow a very common progression from representing only the most prominent sounds in words (semiphonemic spelling) to representing most of the sounds they hear. They also get better at using conventional spelling patterns.

Children typically progress through several phases when developing the ability to hear phonemes in words. First, they represent words with single letters, then they represent both beginning and ending sounds, and finally they detect sounds in the middle of words, and write these too. Consonant sounds are the first to be represented, followed by long vowel sounds, and then short vowel sounds. In English, both consonants and long vowel phonemes are more easily heard as distinct sounds in words than are short vowels.

Teachers should recognize that this progression is most typical of children who are native speakers of English. Children who speak other languages may display a different developmental progression. In Spanish, for example, children's early phonemic spellings often consist mostly of vowels, because most are long in that language, which makes them more prominent than in English. Thus the beginning writing of children who speak Spanish will have a balance of consonant and vowel phonemes represented that is not typical of the early writing of English-speaking children.

It is rare for preschool children to move beyond the beginning stages of semiphonemic spelling. Most will not progress to fully phonemic spelling until kindergarten, and many children will persist with semiphonemic spelling even into first grade. Preschool teachers should be aware of the full progression of early childhood writing development so that they can support the continued growth of all children in their classrooms, wherever they fall on the developmental continuum of emergent writing. Some children will push into the upper levels of the word-making continuum, and a teacher needs to know how to support a child who is progressing to this higher level.

If teachers know what aspect of writing is likely to develop next, they can plan activities and interact with individual children in ways that nudge them toward the next level, no matter where that is on the continuum. For a few children, this means that preschool teachers will help them reach rather sophisticated understandings about how words are made.

The writing samples in Figure 16 illustrate how rapidly these more sophisticated understandings can take hold once children do begin phonemic writing. The figure is composed of six samples drawn in Daniel's daily journal over three weeks' time. Daniel was in kindergarten at the time, which is the typical age at which we would see this kind of writing. In his kindergarten classroom, all children wrote a journal entry each day.

Figure 16
Daniel's Daily Journal

9/10

i ORSWNT NT HDKSL

16a "George went to the castle."

9/10 11

NE SRS MOG

16b "And he saw some ghosts."

NTH MSR   9/14

16c "And the monster."

NU NHTGI   9/15

16d "You know how he got out?"

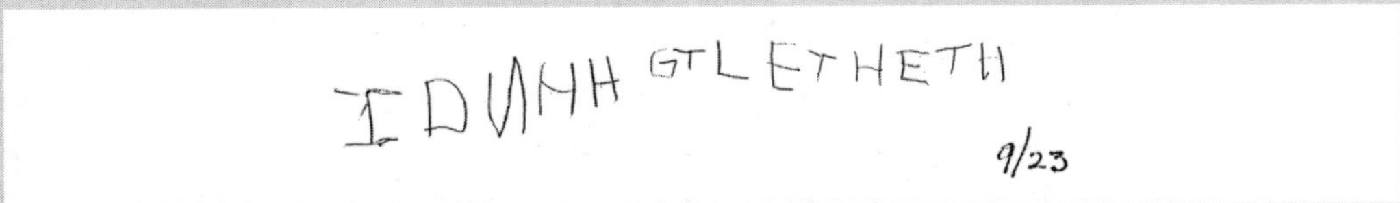

I DNNH GTLETHETN
9/23

16e "I don't know how he got out either."

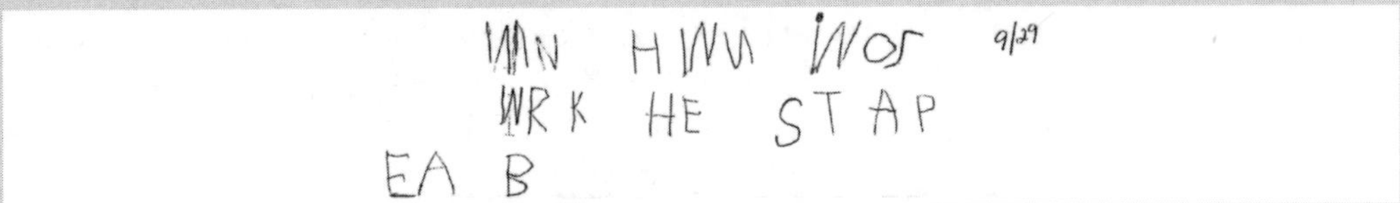

NNN HNN NOT 9/29
NRK HE STAP
EA B

16f "When him was walking, he stepped on a button."

41

Children were free to draw but were also encouraged to write about their pictures. For some children, this writing took the form of single word labels for their drawings. Others, like Daniel, attempted more detailed written descriptions of what was happening in their pictures.

Many aspects of Daniel's writing reflect strategies that preschool teachers begin to see in 5-year-olds who are starting to experiment with phonemic writing. In their struggle to determine which letters to use to represent the sounds they hear in connected speech, many young children have trouble deciding where one word ends and the next begins. Thus they will write without spaces or insert spaces without regard for word boundaries so that their writing looks conventional. This confusion about space and word boundaries is evident in Figures 16a–e.

Even in kindergarten, early phonemic spellers will continue to represent only those sounds that are most prominent in words. This means that they will write using very few vowels, as Daniel did in 16a and 16c, or using only long vowels as he did in 16b and 16e. Short vowel sounds appear only later because they are harder for young children to hear. And even when children try to represent those less prominent sounds, they often choose the wrong vowel letters, as Daniel did in Figure 16f. This occurs primarily because there is less connection between short vowel sounds and letter names, thus rendering the letter name strategy described earlier less useful.

Both preschool and kindergarten children are very likely to occasionally reverse the order of letters in words, as Daniel did in Figure 16b when he spelled *ghosts* with the letters *OG*. While some reversals are due to children imperfectly recalling how a whole word looks as they attempt to write it from memory, resulting in errors like *was* for *saw* for example, other times reversals are directly related to attempts at phonemic spelling. In Daniel's case, his teacher observed him sounding out the word, elongaging the /o/ sound and making it the most prominent. He wrote the *O* and then sounded out the word again, listening for additional sounds. At that point he enunciated the /g/ and promptly added the *G*, apparently satisfied that he had then represented the important sounds in the word.

This kindergarten sample exemplifies the natural progression toward conventional writing that occurs as children move beyond letter strings to the use of real words. While most preschoolers will not progress to this level of phonemic writing, some older preschool children will begin to experiment like Daniel did. Teachers need to become keen observers of children's writing processes in order to fully understand what children are attempting to do and how they arrive at the creations they produce. That understanding will lead to better ability to support preschoolers' writing development.

Summary

The samples in this chapter illustrate just how much children learn about using written language in preschool, and then how much they continue to learn in kindergarten (and beyond). They begin trying to write words by using the letters in their names and copying letters from the environment. Until children figure out that letters are mapped to speech, their words are mock words, nonphonemic letter strings. As children make the connection between sounds and letters, they first represent very few of the sounds they hear, often only the first sound in a word. Gradually, however, they begin to isolate or hear more and more sounds in words they say, and to include more and more letters in their writing to represent this increased phonemic awareness. Finally, but usually not until kindergarten or first grade, children are able to represent most of the sounds that actually make up words.

Teachers can help children become writers by offering opportunities for them to play with language, to explore letters and sounds, and to experiment with writing. Teachers also can write with children, using a process in which words are sounded out and letters used to write the sounds are named as they are written down. Specific ways to structure the classroom to facilitate writing development will be elaborated on in chapter 5.

CHAPTER 4

From Short Messages to Longer and More Coherent Messages

Children's progression from scribbles to script and from letter strings to phonemic spelling tell only part of the story of their development as writers. While they grapple with concepts of symbol formation and the mysteries of word making, they also develop an increasingly sophisticated understanding of how meaning can be conveyed through composition. Children figure out that writing has many purposes and takes many forms. Teachers play a pivotal role in helping children develop this important aspect of writing ability, beginning in preschool.

Oral Composition

The most important thing preschool teachers need to know about message creation is that it begins with **oral language**. Children first learn to compose through talk—whether they tell stories about events in their lives, retell stories from favorite books or television shows, act out story lines in their dramatic play, or tell all about something of interest. As children are encouraged to tell their stories, they are often asked for more information. As Roberto tells about the hedgehog he encountered in the petting zoo, he is likely to be met with a variety of questions: "Did you pet it? What did it feel like? Did it stick you? How big was it? Did the lady feed it? What did it eat?" As Roberto responds, he learns to extend his stories and to include more information. He begins to consider what his audience—his classmates and teacher—will want to know in future stories. Of course, Roberto doesn't consciously consider these aspects of his storytelling. Rather, he and his classmates are socialized into storytelling through their shared interactions. The storytelling skills that they develop, though, are exactly those that they will need when they grow into writing down their stories.

As children are drawn into oral language in preschool classrooms, they begin to internalize the many functions that language can serve. They use their language to describe things and events, such as when they tell stories. They use it to make their needs known and request help. They use it to persuade others to do what they want. They use it to name and label objects in the environment. These are all functions of language that can also be accomplished later through writing. The more varied children's uses are for oral language, the more varied will be their uses of written language. A child who has learned to speak up to ask his classmates to leave his block structure standing will eventually recognize that he can make a sign that says, *Don't knock this down!* A child who wants to tell everyone all about her pet tarantula will discover that she can write a composition about the tarantula to share. What children learn how to do with oral language, they will one day be able to do in writing.

From Oral to Written Composition

There are many ways that teachers can help young children move from oral composition to written expressions of meaning. A language-rich classroom offers a wealth of opportunities for both oral and written expression. **Dramatic play** centers, in particular, give children the chance to explore storytelling as they act out scenarios from their everyday lives or reenact stories that they have learned from books. Equally important, they also create fantasy scenarios in which story lines are developed and plots are carried forward by actions (Edwards, 1990; Kavanaugh & Engle, 1998; McCaslin, 1996). Teachers can extend the language in children's play by participating in it on occasion. One teacher, observing that two children in a veterinarian's office dramatic play center had become quiet and appeared to be losing interest in the roles they were acting out, brought over a stuffed dog and said, "My dog got hit by a car! Can you help?" The children promptly set about examining the dog, giving each other directions for taking X-rays, bandaging a hurt paw, and prescribing medicine for the injured animal. One child even offered advice to the pet owner about keeping her dog from getting out of the yard. By intervening briefly in the children's play, the teacher extended the story they were acting out as well as the language they used.

This play scenario can easily be extended to incorporate experimentation with written language. Centers like a veterinarian's office (or a shoe store, restaurant, or bakery) should be equipped with props that invite writing. A veterinarian's office could include prescription pads, receipts, an appointment book, and a notepad for writing instructions for follow-up care. Children will experiment with these props by using all the forms of writing presented in earlier chapters, ranging from scribbles to letter strings and early phonemic spelling. As is the case for extending the oral language of dramatic play, teachers can also intervene to nudge children toward using the writing props. For example, the teacher who took her dog to the vet could ask the children for a receipt and ask to schedule a follow-up appointment. Doing so helps children experiment with specific functions of writing and encourages children to include writing as a natural part of their pretend play (Christie, 1991; Kieff & Casbergue, 1999).

Figure 17 is an example of the kind of writing that may result when dramatic play centers in preschool classrooms are equipped with appropriate writing materials. Hannah was in a classroom with a well-equipped housekeeping center. One prop was a notepad and a small bulletin board on the "kitchen" counter. Hannah and her friends were acting out a scenario that involved getting ready to go out for the evening and leaving their children with a babysitter. The figure shows a note that Hannah wrote for the babysitter. She began by writing the name of her child, Ben (actually the name of her older brother—a very familiar word indeed). Hannah then explained that she could be reached at the phone number on the first line. Note that she did not write her real phone number, but rather wrote something visually similar to a phone number. It contained six digits and the final digit is a letter rather than a number. The remaining lines of apparent scribble were intended to be instructions for feeding the baby and putting him to bed. Hannah confided that she wrote these in script like her mommy's handwriting. Clearly the dramatic play center and one of the

Figure 17
Hannah's Note to a Babysitter

writing props in it functioned to extend and bring an element of composition into Hannah's play.

While most dramatic play will naturally result in narrative storytelling, it is also important for preschool teachers to foster children's ability to share information and do informational (expository) writing. While some children may naturally engage in sharing information, most will need encouragement to do so. Preschoolers are generally accustomed to talking about their immediate activities and surroundings, and that type of talk is most often carried out in narratives. Informational composition, however, requires children to use a less familiar style of language. This type of writing is best supported when children are provided with lots of content to talk and write about. One of the best ways to engage children with interesting content is to provide a well-equipped **discovery center**. Such a center will contain objects for children to observe and handle (for example, a pet canary in a cage, a birdnest, and some feathers) as well as informational picture books related to those objects. These books should be shared with the children during read-aloud sessions and also displayed in a way that invites children to explore the books themselves while they are in the center. It doesn't matter that the children can't read the books independently. There is much information to be discovered and discussed as they examine the pictures and compare them to the artifacts in the discovery center. Figure 18 shows how simple and inviting such a display can be.

The information children derive from the artifacts and books in the classroom can be shared through both oral and written language. Inviting children to dictate pages to create "all about" books related to specific themes extends both oral language and children's recognition that what they say can be written down. In one preschool classroom, the 4-year-olds spent three weeks studying "creepy crawlies." The discovery center contained an aquarium housing a tarantula on loan from one of the families; a Japanese cricket cage with a live cricket, also from a child's home; and a variety of insects mounted in magnifying boxes purchased from a teaching supply store. Children went on "bug hunts" in the play yard to find out where different creatures liked to live and to observe them in their natural habitats and shared many books with their teachers about insects, spiders, worms, and centipedes. Periodically throughout this time of exploration, children were invited to dictate information about their favorite creatures for inclusion in a class book. As can be seen in the following examples, children's contributions ranged from simple phrases to detailed descriptions, with many children including more information for later dictations than for earlier ones.

Figure 18
Discovery Center Display

Caitlin: Butterflies. They fly and they eat other bugs. And they eat plants. They lay their eggs on plants.

Eric: Lizard. I like a lizard.

Gabriella: Doodlebugs always roll up when you touch them. They always tickle when they're on your hand.

Kate: Snakes. I like purple ones and rattlesnakes and milk snakes and coral snakes.

Leo: Ladybugs. They spit a yellow liquid so birds can't eat them. They eat bad bugs. They eat leaves. They're red and orange. They have a back with spots and red.

Max: I like spiders. And I like spider webs too. I like spiders when they're on the spider webs.

Tyrone: Ladybugs. I learned about not mush them. To hold them careful. They live in the grass. They eat those green bugs.

Written Composition

While it is clear from the preschoolers' dictations shown previously that some children are very verbal and have lots to say about topics in which they have an interest, it is also clear, upon examining these children's written attempts, that their writing lags behind their oral language. This is typical. Just as babies can understand many more words than they are able to say, so too can preschoolers construct oral compositions that are more sophisticated than they can convey in writing.

The writing sample in Figure 19 is Christopher's attempt to write his own page for the class book about insects. He read it to his teacher as follows: "Spiders. Poison. Spiders live on rocks." Christopher indicated that the objects on the left in his composition were rocks and spider webs, while other lines were the words. While he had not yet developed a conventional understanding of writing, he was beginning to develop a good sense of how to convey information about a specific topic.

Figure 19
Christopher's Page for an Insect Book

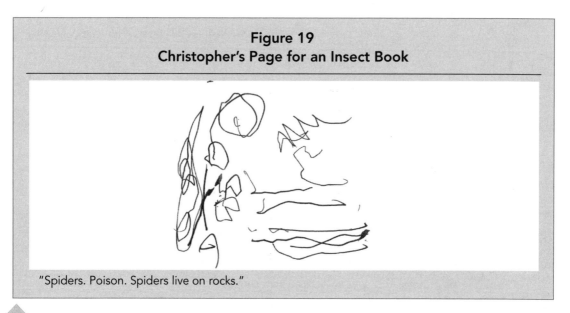

"Spiders. Poison. Spiders live on rocks."

Figure 20
Emily's Flower Story

The gap between what children can write and their oral composition
ability is equally evident in their narratives. Figure 20 represents 4-year-old
Emily's story about a flower. The only conventional writing in this sample
is her name. She asked her teacher to write down the story that went with
her picture, signaling an understanding of the difference between drawing
and writing. Emily's dictations revealed that she was developing into a
competent storyteller:

> Once upon a time, there was a flower. It was snowing and it froze to death.
> It didn't have any water forever and ever. And then one day it did get some
> water because the person saw it wasn't going to get any water. "Mom, our
> flower did get some." And along came an ant that said, "I'm going to eat you,

flower." But the ant was joking. And I hope you feel better flower because it's still freezing but it did get water. The flower felt better because it found a lake and thought it would be fun.

While the plot of her story is somewhat disjointed, it is clear that Emily understood that stories have conflict—in this case a flower freezing to death without water and being threatened by an ant—and that stories end when the conflict is resolved. While she didn't yet have the ability to write her story using print, she was nonetheless successful at composition.

When children have stories to tell, and first begin to write using print exclusively, they often struggle to get meaning onto paper. Remember how Daniel's writing in the previous chapter (Figure 16) revealed his struggles to figure out how to spell words? Figure 21 illustrates that he also struggled with how to represent meaning in his writing and grappled with what constitutes a story, gradually building on an abbreviated form until he was able to at least include a brief introduction, problem, and resolution.

In Figure 21a, written during the third week of kindergarten, Daniel was able to write only "Once upon a time Daniel" as his full composition. Six weeks later (21b), he built on that simple introduction to write, "Once upon a time there was a werewolf." He continued this pattern for quite a while, as in 21c, when he wrote, "Once upon a time there was a yellow egg." Each of these journal entries described a picture he drew on a separate page.

In subsequent entries, however, he began to expand this format, as can be seen in 21d, when he wrote, "Once upon a time there was the rocket. It blasted off." Here, he used the familiar form to describe his picture of a rocket but then elaborated action for the rocket. Figure 21e followed the same pattern of basic description followed by elaboration: "Once upon a time there was a ghost and the ghost was covered (with slime)." It wasn't until later in the school year (21f) that his own storytelling voice came through in his writing as he wrote, "Once upon a time there was a ghost. And you know what that ghost did? He climbed in a tree." All along, Daniel's pictures were filled with the elements of the fantasy stories and cartoons that he loved, and he was able to talk about those pictures at length. But the ability to write those stories with print was slow to catch up. Given that the gap between the stories children are able to tell and the actual writing they are able to do persists well into kindergarten and even first grade, preschool teachers should not be at all discouraged that children in their classrooms represent so little of what they say on paper. While most preschool teachers are unlikely to see the kind of story writing demonstrated by Daniel, they

Figure 21
Daniel's Story Writing Progress

WT PRT DANIEL   9/3

21a "Once upon a time Daniel"

10/29

WS put thi WZEWF

21b "Once upon a time there was a werewolf."

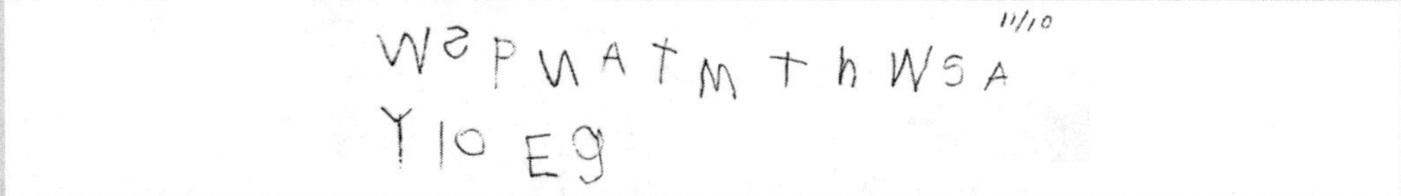

WƏPNATM t h WSA ⁱⁱ/₁₀
Y ₁₀ Eg

21c "Once upon a time there was a yellow egg."

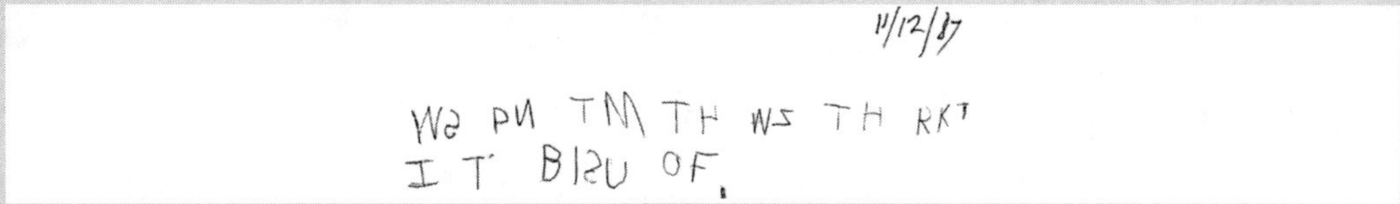

11/12/87

WƏ PN TM TH WS TH RKT
I T BlƏU OF.

21d "Once upon a time there was the rocket. It blasted off."

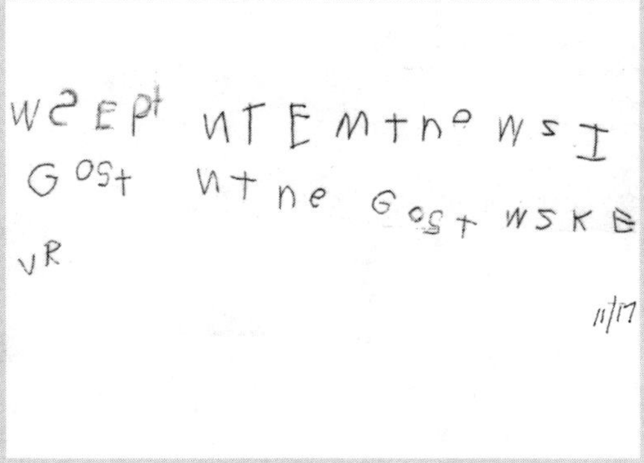

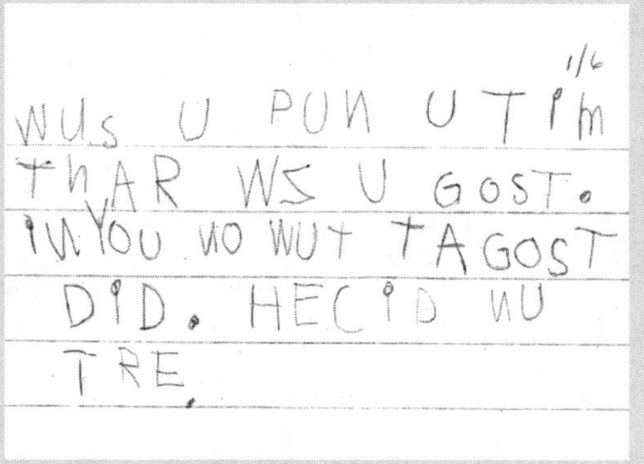

WƏ EP⁺ NTE M t nº WS I
G ᵒˢ⁺ Nt ne G ᵒˢ⁺ WSK B
ᵥR   11/17

21e "Once upon a time there was a ghost and the ghost was covered (with slime)."

WUS U PUN U TiM ¹/₆
ThAR WS U GOST.
IN YOU NO WUT TA GOST
DID. HE CiD NU
TRE.

21f "Once upon a time there was a ghost. And you know what that ghost did? He climbed in a tree."

53

should recognize that their persistent efforts to extend children's oral language and encourage them to experiment with writing will benefit children when they are ready to begin writing their stories themselves.

Summary

The samples of children's oral and written compositions in this chapter offer compelling evidence that young children are capable of constructing meaningful stories and informational pieces. Their ability to do this can be supported by teachers who provide lots of opportunities for both oral language and writing in their classrooms. Children can express themselves through their dramatic play, with skillful teachers extending the scenarios they act out and providing materials that will encourage writing as a natural part of their pretense.

Teachers can further enhance children's oral and written language abilities by engaging them with content that they will find interesting. The more children have to talk about, the more they will eventually have to write about—whether that writing is dictated to teachers or written independently. Classrooms filled with interesting objects, books, and activities will invite children to talk—to their parents, to their teachers, and to each other. And with the support of caring teachers, all that language can be funneled into opportunities for children to engage with written language.

CHAPTER 5

Time, Space, Materials, and a Helping Hand

Although it was not our focus in earlier chapters, it has probably occurred to you that each of the samples of children's writing provided in this book took a certain amount of time, occurred in a specific physical context, and required some materials. Many of these writing attempts also involved direct interaction with an adult. Preschool children like to write, will write a lot, and will learn a lot about writing, but only if there is an environment that supports this type of activity (Neuman & Roskos, 1992; Twardosz, Roskos, & Lenhart, 2003). In this short chapter, we discuss the settings for many of the examples we have already considered.

Looking Across the Examples

One way to consider the context in which young children's writing occurs is to analyze a number of samples in terms of the time and place of their occurrence and the material and social resources involved in their creation. Table 1 provides an overview of many of the examples included in earlier chapters.

One thing that stands out in the summary table is that the children's writing was produced in a setting where writing was encouraged and supported with materials and time. Whether at home or at school, children were provided with specific materials and given time to engage with them. In the home samples, writing materials were provided by the parent as a way to occupy the child while the parent was busy working in the kitchen or office. The child wanted something to do and also wanted to be near the parent. On many of these occasions, the parent occupied the child with writing materials and interacted with the child while working. (On other occasions, the parent provided play dough, puzzles, toy figures, or small blocks, or found some way for the child to help with food preparation.) Many of the writing creations ended up on the family's refrigerator door for display, along with paintings and drawings. The child sometimes showed these to family members and to other adults who visited.

Table 1
Physical and Social Support for Children's Writing

Example	Physical Context	Materials	Child's Purpose	Adult Involvement
Figure 1a	Home, kitchen table	Small notepad	Experimenting with letter forms and arrangement on a page	Parent (working in kitchen) suggested activity, made occasional suggestions while child was writing; when child finished, asked child to "tell me about it"
Figure 1b	Preschool writing center; early in day when writing and several other centers were open for 30 minutes of child-choice time	Single sheets of paper and simple blank books; markers and colored pencils	Creating the look of a storybook; playing with writing; used large single sheets of paper and a black marker	Occasional teacher interaction to comment and ask questions ("tell me about that"); child gave some pages to teacher when finished and put rest of book in take-home folder
Figure 2	Home, dining room table	Small notepad paper, thin blue marker	Experimenting with lines; larger purpose was to be in same room with parent who was working nearby	Parent suggested activity and interacted occasionally, responding when child said, "Look," and commenting about lines
Figure 3a	Preschool writing center	Blue construction paper and blue marker selected from variety of paper and markers provided in writing center	Experimenting with word making; started with known word (DADA) and then combined letters to create other "words"	Occasional interaction with teachers about "writing a lot of words"
Figure 3b	Preschool housekeeping center	Pad of white paper and marker placed by toy telephone	Taking phone message as part of dramatic play	Teacher sometimes answered phone, took message, and then delivered it to children who were playing

(continued)

Table 1 (continued)

Example	Physical Context	Materials	Child's Purpose	Adult Involvement
Figure 3c	Preschool classroom block area	Sheets of paper, markers, clipboard, masking tape	Writing signature on paper taped to block structure to signal it was not to be taken down by other players during activity period	Teacher prompted child to make sign to preserve building
Figure 3d	Preschool art table	Construction paper for collages, markers, set of class name cards on ring binder	Writing signature on back of collage to indicate ownership	Teacher asked children to sign their collages; provided child's name card and read letters from card; child (2 years, 10 months) scribbled to write signature and did not stop until teacher had stopped reading letters in child's name
Figure 4a	Home, on workroom table	White paper	Playing with lines; occupying self with materials parent was using	Parent suggested activity and looked when child wanted to show something; commented occasionally about interesting lines and shapes; asked about scribbles in lower right; responded "I love you, too," when child conveyed message
Figure 4b	Preschool art center; child's picture with name written at bottom and upper left	Construction paper and markers	Drawing picture; writing name to indicate ownership	Occasional interaction as children drew pictures; teacher asked children to sign pictures

(continued)

Table 1 (continued)

Example	Physical Context	Materials	Child's Purpose	Adult Involvement
Figure 6c	Preschool writing center	Assorted paper and writing tools	Experimenting; practicing letters and letterlike forms	Occasional comments by teacher about how hard child was working
Figure 7	Preschool writing center	Paper cut into "tickets"; variety of markers; word cards with *Three Little Pigs*, *ticket*, and so forth written on them	Making tickets for class play; parents and other family members invited to attend play a few days hence	Teacher offered ticketmaking as choice for activity time; assisted children by helping them use word cards and modeling letter formation
Figure 8b	Preschool block area	Paper, markers, clipboard, masking tape	Making sign for library built as part of block city	Child asked teacher how to write (spell) *library*; teacher sounded out word, and child matched letter to all sounds except final sound (teacher dictated letter Y); teacher advised about placement of second line of print, but child rejected advice
Figure 9a–c	Preschool writing center	Strips of paper provided for writing names of color swatches saved from color-mixing activity at art table	Labeling color swatches for a class book	Teacher set task and helped children write (spell) words; modeled letter formation when requested; sounded out words to help children spell; dictated letters when child's letter-name match strategy was not effective
Figure 14	Preschool writing center	Paper, markers	Making a birthday greeting card for a classmate	Teacher asked what message said; child "read" it to her

(continued)

Table 1 (continued)

Example	Physical Context	Materials	Child's Purpose	Adult Involvement
Figure 16a–f	Kindergarten classroom, daily journal entry writing time	Individual journal, pencil	Assignment from teacher to make journal entry each day	Teacher observed child occasionally and listened as child read each finished entry aloud; sometimes took dictation in "grown-up" writing and placed it on corresponding page with sticky note
Figure 17	Preschool housekeeping center	Notepad and small bulletin board on counter in play kitchen, marker	Playing mommy; leaving instructions for babysitter	Teacher observed interaction and heard child read/explain note to child playing babysitter
Figure 19	Preschool classroom writing center and thematic discovery center	Oversize paper for class book, pencils, markers	Contributing to class book about insects	Teacher planned thematic unit to provide information and spark interest; set task and provided blank pages; took dictation about favorite creepy-crawly creatures; spent time in both learning centers; placed completed book in library center
Figure 20	Preschool writing center	Drawing paper, markers	Writing a story about a flower	Teacher took dictation and read the story back to child; child taped dictation to her picture and took both home to share with parents

In the preschool samples, writing materials were provided in a learning center devoted specifically to writing (and to the drawing that invariably accompanies much of a young child's writing), and also in areas such as the block area, art area, and **dramatic play** center, where writing is a logical element of play. Without these provisions, children would not have been prompted to write.

A second characteristic of the children's writing was that their purpose was often to experiment with lines—children were playing with writing or practicing some aspect of writing. This kind of play and self-directed practice is essential for the preschool child. With access to a **writing center** for much of the day, children were free to engage in this self-selected activity.

On other occasions, the writing center was the setting for activities in which the teacher, not the child, set the purpose for writing. The writing samples shown in Figures 7, 9, 16, and 19 were produced under such circumstances. The first three samples related to group projects—a production of *The Three Little Pigs*, the making of a class book on colors, and the making of a class book about creepy crawlies—and took over the writing center for a period of time. The other teacher-suggested sample (Figure 16) was an individual journal-writing activity.

Some writing center activities require more adult time and attention than others. In the case of the tickets and the color class book, a teacher was stationed in the writing center during activity time to support children in their writing efforts. At other times (about 80% of the time), when a specific activity was not planned for the writing center, teachers floated among learning centers. Adult interactions with children around their writing were much more frequent when specific projects were planned for the writing center. Not surprisingly, children also asked for more help with their writing on these occasions, in part, no doubt, because the writing they produced was for "the public," not just for themselves.

Although the greatest amount of adult–child interaction, and thus instruction about writing, occurred when specific teacher-suggested projects were placed in the writing center, the notes in the far-right column of Table 1 indicate that teachers also provided instruction in contexts where children themselves set purposes for their writing. If we look at Figure 8b, we see that a child playing in the block area wanted to make a sign and enlisted the teacher's help. The teacher sounded out the word, which the child could not do on her own, and she helped the child with one of the sound–letter matches. Countless previous interactions with adults, both at school and at home, were involved in this child's acquisition of letter-name knowledge, her understanding that letters represent sounds in words, and her skill in writing letters. On this occasion, she demonstrated independence in some aspects of writing and asked for help when needed. We see the same thing in Figure 20. The child wanted to write a story. Although she composed it, she could not write it all down. Her teacher joined her at the writing center to take dictation as the child told her story. Young children often cannot orchestrate all aspects of writing at the same time. For example, they may be able to compose orally but unable to write down everything they have said. In these instances, the parent or teacher scaffolds the task by helping with a specific aspect of it, as the teacher did here by physically writing the story for the child.

Setting the Stage and Directing the Action

Physical stage-setting is essential if we are to encourage preschoolers to write. Teachers must provide places and materials for children to write and must allocate time for children to engage in writing. These are indirect, but powerful, ways that teachers use to guide children toward engagement with writing. More direct encouragement for writing comes when teachers suggest that children make signs for block buildings, ask them to write names on drawings and paintings, introduce a simple sign-out system for books in a lending library, establish a system of learning center sign-up sheets that require children's signatures, explain various writing props, and model uses of writing in dramatic play. Some of these occasions for writing (e.g., names on pictures, names on book check-out cards, and names on sign-up sheets) constitute classroom routines. In other words, these practices become so much a part of how life is conducted in the classroom that children engage in them as a matter of course. They become what Twardosz, Roskos, and Lenhart (2003) refer to as **symbolic resources**. These are community and cultural ways of doing things that simply become part of children's lives.

A second kind of direct encouragement of writing is provided when teachers set up specific writing projects that connect in some way with ongoing classroom units of study. In these, the teacher sets the task, although each child's specific contribution to the class project varies considerably, depending on the child's level of skill and individual ideas about how to contribute.

The younger the preschool child, the more important it is to provide mostly indirect encouragement and support for writing, and to encourage writing as a part of routines. As children approach the later preschool years (4 $\frac{1}{2}$ to 5 $\frac{1}{2}$ years of age), teachers can add more activities that involve direct encouragement of writing. As preschoolers mature, they become more social, and engage in more cooperative play with their peers. We see this in dramatic play, in block play, and in projects that children sometimes set for themselves at the writing table. Recall from the introduction the story *FIRE FIRE*, which was written by two young 5-year-olds during the spring of their second year of preschool. Projects that a teacher provides occasionally for the writing center (e.g., class books to which children contribute a page or two) can build on this budding social development that is seen in the older preschool child.

It is important to provide a variety of writing situations and activities in the preschool classroom. The balance found among the kinds of opportunities provided for writing will shift as preschoolers get older. Teachers strive to create the balance that works best for the current interests and skills of the children in their classrooms.

CHAPTER 6

Home–School Connections and Ideas for Assessment

Educators at every level are faced with increasing calls for accountability, which often translate into pressure to assess children's learning. In the United States, federal mandates have focused a spotlight on literacy learning and heightened discussion about the importance of ensuring that all children arrive at kindergarten ready to benefit from the more focused literacy instruction that characterizes a move from preschool to formal schooling.

Preschool teachers, too, must assess children's progress. While they are rarely required to administer formal, standardized assessments, they should be aware of each child's progress so that they can design teacher-directed instruction as well as play opportunities that accommodate children's varying abilities. At the preschool level, the best way to do this is to carefully observe and document children's demonstrations of growth. In terms of writing development, that means taking note of the varied ways that children attempt to write and preserving their drawing and writing so that development over time can be documented.

Teachers must always keep in mind, however, that the writing they see in the classroom tells only part of the story of a child's capabilities. The drawing and writing that children do at home can add rich information to the overall picture of children's literacy development. Some children produce more writing at home than they do at school; for some, the home setting may inspire different purposes for writing. Enlisting parents and other primary caregivers as partners in assessing and supporting preschoolers' writing development helps everyone involved develop a better understanding of how a child understands the functions, forms, and meanings of written language.

Engaging the adults in children's lives as full participants in the assessment and support of their preschoolers' literacy promotes a respectful view of families by acknowledging that all families have strengths that can be tapped to help children achieve (Rockwell, Andre, & Hawley, 1996). As teachers communicate with parents and other caregivers about children's literacy development, they gain insight into family situations that help shape children's learning. They also learn more about what prompts children to write at home, which provides insight as to how they can adapt classroom activities to work well with diverse populations.

Strategies for Home and School Assessment

Because the most appropriate literacy assessment procedures for young children are informal and observational (Morrow & Smith, 1990), there need be little difference between what teachers do at school and what they ask parents to do at home. In both settings, children's attempts to write should be observed and samples of their writing shared and discussed. Most parents and caregivers are eager to share stories about their children. Teachers can encourage parents to watch for any signs of drawing and writing that the children do at home and ask them to bring in samples and take a minute to describe what they observed while the child was writing. The sample in Figure 22 was brought to school by Hannah's mother, who had watched and listened while the 3-year-old gathered stuffed animals and dolls and proceeded to conduct a meeting, taking notes on a stenographer's pad borrowed from her mom's desk.

Figure 22
Hannah's First Set of "Meeting Minutes"

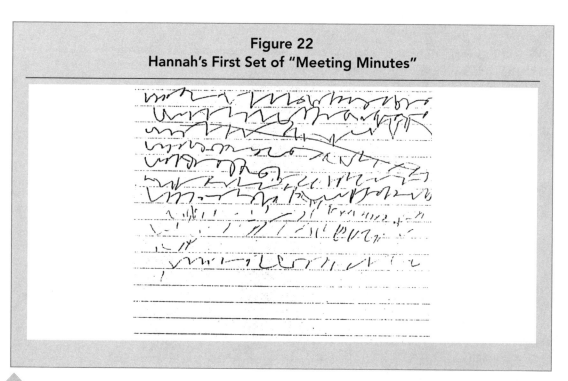

Figure 23
Hannah's Second Set of "Meeting Minutes"

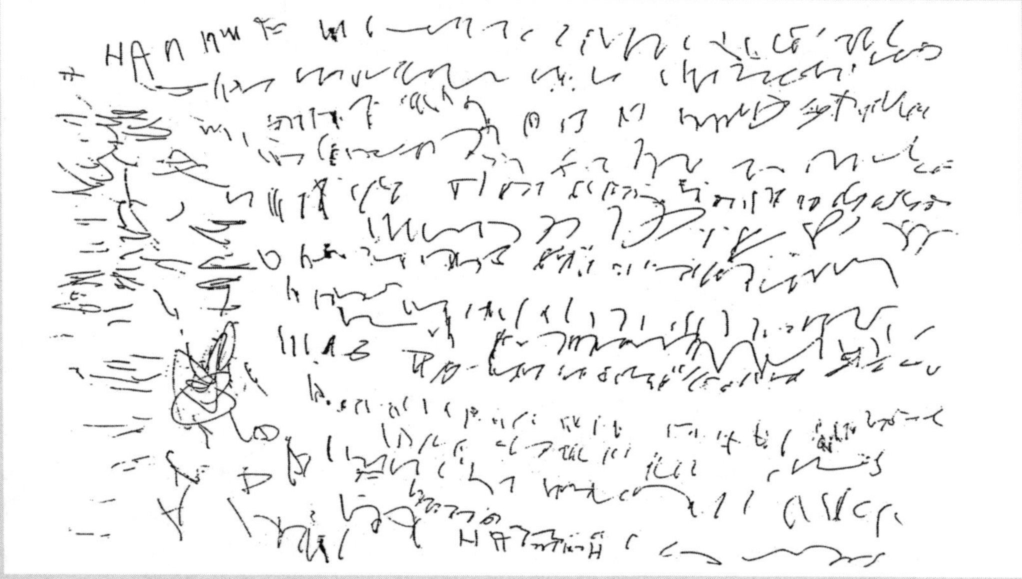

Hannah's "minutes" from her meeting are a series of linear scribbles. During a brief interaction when Hannah's mother dropped her off at school in the morning, Hannah's teacher was able to point out that Hannah knew that writing was done in lines from left to right, and that she knew that writing could be used to write down things that should be remembered, such as an important discussion at a meeting. It wasn't long after this that Hannah's mom sent in the sample in Figure 23 with a note that said, "Hannah had another meeting." When she picked up Hannah that afternoon, the mother was quick to point out that Hannah had attempted to write her name at the top of the page. The teacher then pointed out that, unlike in the first sample, Hannah this time had written a series of separate figures, suggesting that she had made an important discovery about print—that it is composed of distinct letters. The teacher drew the mother's attention to what appeared to be Hannah's name, again printed at the bottom of the page. She also pointed out that the writing on the left side of the page appeared to move in a different direction than the rest of the lines and explained that children Hannah's age often use space on a page creatively, turning the paper to fill up empty margins when they run out of space at the bottom. Hannah's mother confirmed that she had often seen Hannah turning her papers around and around as she wrote, and both women laughingly agreed that Hannah must have had a long meeting.

The pleasurable, collaborative sharing of stories about Hannah's writing exemplifies the type of interaction with parents and other caregivers that teachers should try to have. Hannah's teacher set up a "parents' corner" in her classroom—a bulletin board just inside the door on which she posted copies of notes to be sent home; pages for parents to sign up to help in the classroom or chaperone outings; and space for parents to post pictures and artifacts from home that they wanted to share with children, teachers, and other parents. When writing samples were brought in, the teacher summarized the parent's story of the writing and placed a copy of the sample along with the summary in a folder for the child. The original sample was then posted on the parents' corner display. This process served two important purposes. First, it allowed the teacher to capture a picture of the children's home literacy to which she could return later for comparison. Second, it demonstrated the importance of all forms of writing to everyone who perused the board. As some parents brought in samples, it encouraged others to watch for similar efforts in their own homes and helped them to value the ways that preschoolers experiment with writing. Perhaps the desire to see their own children represented on the board even prompted some parents to provide their children with writing materials and to engage in writing with them.

Establishing comfortable routines for sharing stories of literacy development can help parents and other caregivers feel comfortable enough with the teacher to discuss concerns they might have about their children's writing. Parents are sometimes unduly concerned that their children are at risk for later difficulty with literacy learning. Backward letters or other errors in **directionality**, for example, often cause parents to worry that their children might have a learning disability. Teachers can assure parents that letter reversals and inconsistent directionality are perfectly normal during the preschool years, and in fact persist for many letters well into first and second grades.

The coloring book pages shown in Figure 24 might have been cause for concern had Daniel's mother not been aware of the normal course of writing development. Three-year-old Daniel colored the page on the left

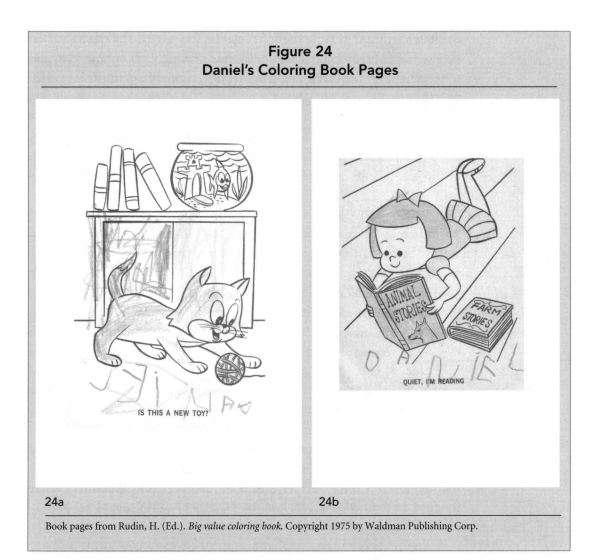

Figure 24
Daniel's Coloring Book Pages

IS THIS A NEW TOY?

ANIMAL STORIES

FARM STORIES

QUIET, I'M READING

24a   24b

Book pages from Rudin, H. (Ed.). *Big value coloring book.* Copyright 1975 by Waldman Publishing Corp.

(24a) by himself at home and then wrote his name on the bottom from right to left, reversing most of the letters. At his request, his aunt colored the page on the right. When both had finished coloring, Daniel proclaimed that his aunt's coloring was better and promptly signed his name to that picture too, this time writing from left to right (24b). When his teacher saw this sample and heard the story of how it was produced, she was able to point out that Daniel was probably using solid logic to determine how to write his name in the coloring book. The rule seemed to be not to start from the left, but to start from the center binding of the pages and work out from there. She also marveled with the mother at his ability to visually flip the letters around to write them. Daniel's mom laughed as she described Daniel taking credit for his aunt's coloring by affixing his name to it, and the teacher pointed out that Daniel seemed to understand the powerful function that writing his name can serve. The teacher's note about this brief sharing session included the fact that Daniel was coloring with his aunt, a sign that extended family was involved in his literacy development. She was sure to post this sample in the parents' corner, knowing that it would provide lots of opportunities to reassure other parents about backward writing.

As mentioned earlier, the parents' corner in this classroom also allowed parents or other primary caregivers to post pictures of the children engaged in activities at home or on outings with their families. Photographs of special events such as a new brother's bris to celebrate his Jewish heritage or a Japanese child's celebration of Children's Day with his siblings prompted both parents and children to share stories from their lives. Children were encouraged to tell about who was in the pictures and what was happening, leading to the kind of oral storytelling that we discussed in chapter 4. The teacher also encouraged parents to bring in pictures of more ordinary days in their children's lives as a way of affirming the value of everyday family interaction. Recognizing that not all families had the means to take and develop photographs, she sought the donation of an easy-to-operate camera and then sent it and a roll of 12-exposure film home with a different family each week. She asked parents to try to "catch" their children reading and writing at home. Parents who could develop the film on their own did so, and the teacher set aside part of her supply budget to develop film for the other families.

Figure 25 is a photo brought in by Emily's mother. Emily and her classmate Stephanie often spent weekend days together, and one of their favorite pastimes was drawing, painting, and writing. The photograph shows them absorbed with their writing efforts, working amid a variety of paints, paper, and markers arrayed on the kitchen table.

Figure 26 is one writing sample that Emily's mother brought in to accompany the picture. She described how Emily and Stephanie both contributed to it, alternately drawing and writing, using a variety of scribbles, mock letters, a signature, and other actual letters. This sample provided yet another chance for the teacher to demonstrate that all of these forms of writing were valued. Its placement on the board prompted other parents to bring in similar samples that they might not have recognized as important before seeing the bulletin board display.

Figure 25
Children "Caught" Writing at Home

Figure 26
Emily and Stephanie's Collaborative Writing

Figure 27
Hannah's Third Writing Sample

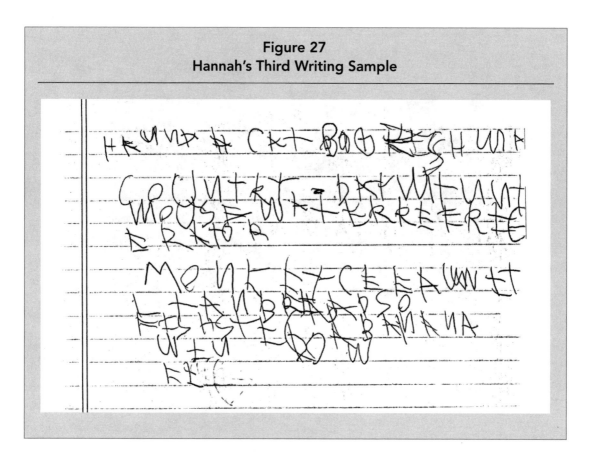

When teachers and parents begin to collaborate about literacy development early in children's lives, many parents will carry the expectation for that sort of involvement forward as their children move into other classrooms and then enter kindergarten. These expectations empower parents to advocate for their children and remain involved in their learning. Hannah's parents demonstrated this when Hannah turned 4 and graduated to a new preschool class. Assuming that the new teacher would also want to share observations about Hannah's writing, the child's mother brought in the sample in Figure 27 without waiting for the teacher to ask. Luckily, the teacher was happy to discuss the sample with her and learned that Hannah and her dad had written it together at Hannah's request. At this point in her development, Hannah had become aware that writing is done with letters; she spent lots of time both at home and at school practicing writing letters. She knew that words have correct spellings and often asked adults around her to spell words for her to write. Hannah's mother reported that her husband had provided all the conventional spellings evident in this piece, while Hannah wrote some words herself, with no effort to map sound to letters. Examining this writing sample with Hannah's parents gave the teacher a glimpse into Hannah's home life. She could see that Hannah's literacy efforts were well supported at home. Adding a copy of this sample and a summary of her conversation with Hannah's mother to Hannah's writing folder provided valuable assessment information. As the folder was filled over the course of the school year with additional samples from home and school, a clear picture of Hannah's growth emerged.

Challenges to Collaboration

Teachers who hope to involve parents in observing, documenting, and sharing their preschoolers' experimentation with writing must be prepared to face a number of challenges. They must recognize that differences in culture, family composition, literacy levels, language, and even beliefs about how children become literate will impact how parents and caregivers interact with teachers (Lilly & Green, 2003). Teachers need to carefully examine their own assumptions about parents' and caregivers' roles in their children's education and make sure that any preconceived ideas about families' literacy activities are set aside so that they are open to hearing family stories of literate behavior and finding the strengths in what is shared (Kieff & Wellhousen, 2000). This is especially true if the behaviors described don't fit the teacher's beliefs about what home literacy should look like.

Daniel's teacher, for example, frowns on coloring books, preferring open-ended art activities. When Daniel's mother brought in the coloring book pages in Figure 24, his teacher could have used the opportunity to suggest that encouraging the child to color on blank paper might be a better activity. But to do so would ignore the fact that the child engaged in a valid and valuable literacy interaction with his aunt as part of the coloring book activity. The teacher's choice not to include coloring books in her own classroom does not negate the fact that in many homes, those books offer opportunities for wonderful interaction between parents and children.

Computer use is another area in which the views of early childhood teachers may be at odds with those of many families. Most early childhood educators agree that there are few benefits to allowing children to spend independent, unstructured time in front of a computer screen, especially when that activity replaces more active play that promotes interaction, oral language, and exploration with drawing and writing. Computers are becoming commonplace in many homes, however, and parents often encourage their preschoolers to spend time with programs designed to foster early literacy. Rather than voicing disapproval of computer use in general, teachers can help parents put computer use into perspective and make sure that parents consider what type of computer activity is age appropriate. In terms of writing, most preschoolers will probably benefit most from simply playing with a keyboard in an open-ended word-processing program. If an adult sets the program to use a large font, children can experiment with typing letters and watching them appear on the screen. Parents can join in this play and name letters for children as they appear, thus helping them attend to discrete features of print.

Finally, teachers may discover that because of the pressure parents feel to get their children ready for kindergarten, some may have unreasonable expectations for their children's literacy development. Some parents worry that their children aren't developing at a proper rate; others may pressure teachers to engage children in activities that are not appropriate for their development. This is why it is important for preschool teachers to understand what can be expected of children at different phases of their development. The previous chapters provide a guide to the typical progression children make, from exploring how to make marks to composing meaning with letters mapped onto sounds; teachers can share this information with parents to help them interpret their children's literacy development.

For more information regarding what is developmentally appropriate, teachers can turn to sources like *Learning to Read and Write: Developmentally Appropriate Practices for Young Children* (International Reading Association & National Association for the Education of Young Children, 1998). This position statement includes expectations for children's literacy achievement at different ages, beginning in preschool, and suggests a variety of activities that will support that achievement. Also, a national panel on preventing reading difficulties led to the development of a guide for promoting children's early literacy that includes developmental expectations and supportive activities for parents and teachers (Burns, Griffin, & Snow, 1999).

The Promise of Home–School Partnerships

Despite the challenges teachers face in collaborating with parents to assess and support preschoolers' writing development, the results are worth the effort. All parents, regardless of their own literacy levels, can offer insight into how children engage in writing outside the classroom. Bringing parents into frequent conversations about their children and sharing the joys and concerns embedded in their stories can unite teachers and families in their resolve to do what is best for individual children. These exchanges also provide opportunities for teachers and parents to develop an appreciation for each other's perspectives on children's learning. Perhaps this will lead to families bringing more of the literacy interactions that occur at school into their homes. Equally important, it may lead teachers to provide opportunities and interactions that more closely match those that children are comfortable with from their home environments.

REFERENCES

Baghban, M. (1984). *Our daughter learns to read and write: A case study from birth to 3.* Newark, DE: International Reading Association.

Burns, M.S., Griffin, P., & Snow, C. (Eds.). (1999). *Starting out right: A guide to promoting children's reading success.* Washington, DC: National Academy Press.

Calkins, L.M. (1994). *The art of teaching writing.* Portsmouth, NH: Heinemann.

Christie, J.F. (Ed.). (1991). *Play and early literacy development.* Albany: State University of New York Press.

Clay, M.M. (1975). *What did I write? Beginning reading behaviour.* Portsmouth, NH: Heinemann.

Clay, M.M. (1987). *Writing begins at home: Preparing children for writing before they go to school.* Portsmouth, NH: Heinemann.

Edwards, L.C. (1990). *Affective development and the creative arts: A process approach to early childhood education.* Columbus, OH: Merrill.

Fields, M.V. (1998). *Your child learns to read and write.* Olney, MD: Association for Childhood Education International.

International Reading Association, & National Association for the Education of Young Children. (1998). *Learning to read and write: Developmentally appropriate practices for young children.* Newark, DE: Author; Washington, DC: Author.

Invernizzi, M. (2003). Concepts, sounds, and the ABCs: A diet for the very young reader. In D.M. Barone & L.M. Morrow (Eds.), *Literacy and young children: Research-based practices* (pp. 140–156). New York: Guilford.

Kavanaugh, R., & Engle, S. (1998). The development of pretense and narrative in early childhood. In O.N. Saracho & B. Spodek (Eds.), *Multiple perspectives on play in early childhood education* (pp. 80–99). Albany: State University of New York Press.

Kieff, J.E., & Casbergue, R.M. (1999). *Playful learning and teaching: Integrating play into preschool and primary programs.* Boston: Allyn & Bacon.

Kieff, J., & Wellhousen, K. (2000). Planning family involvement in early childhood programs. *Young Children, 55*(3), 18–25.

Lilly, E., & Green, C. (2003). *Developing partnerships with families through children's literature.* Upper Saddle River, NJ: Pearson.

McCaslin, N. (1996). *Creative drama in the classroom and beyond* (6th ed.). White Plains, NY: Longman.

Morrow, L.M., & Smith, J.K. (1990). *Assessment for instruction in early literacy.* Englewood Cliffs, NJ: Prentice Hall.

Neuman, S.B., & Roskos, K. (1992). The influence of literacy-enriched play settings on preschoolers' engagement with written language. In J. Zutell & S. McCormick (Eds.), *Literacy theory and research: Analyses from multiple paradigms* (41st yearbook of the National Reading Conference, pp. 179–187). Chicago: National Reading Conference.

Raffi. (1985). Apples and bananas. On *One Light, One Sun* [CD]. Cambridge, MA: Rounder Records.

Rockwell, R., Andre, L., & Hawley, M. (1996). *Parents and teachers as partners: A guide for early childhood educators.* Fort Worth, TX: Harcourt College.

Schickedanz, J.A. (1990). *Adam's righting revolutions: One child's literacy development from infancy through grade one.* Portsmouth, NH: Heinemann.

Twardosz, S., Roskos, K., & Lenhart, L. (2003, May). *Optimizing learning opportunities in classrooms: Arranging the resources of the environment to support early literacy instruction in pre-K–2.* Paper presented at the 48th annual convention of the International Reading Association, Orlando, FL.

INDEX

Note: Page numbers followed by *f* and *t* indicate figures and tables, respectively.

A

B–C

D

E

F–G